Strategies for High Performance Organizations— The CEO Report

Employee Involvement, TQM, and Reengineering Programs in Fortune 1000 Corporations

Edward E. Lawler III
with Susan Albers Mohrman
and Gerald E. Ledford Jr.

Jossey-Bass Publishers • San Francisco

Jossey-Bass books and products are available through most bookstores. To contact Jossey-Bass directly, call (888) 378-2537, fax to (800) 605-2665, or visit our website at www.josseybass.com.

Substantial discounts on bulk quantities of Jossey-Bass books are available to corporations, professional associations, and other organizations. For details and discount information, contact the special sales department at Jossey-Bass.

For sales outside the United States, please contact your local Simon & Schuster International Office.

Manufactured in the United States of America.

Library of Congress Cataloging-in-Publication Data

Lawler, Edward E.
    Strategies for high performance organizations : the CEO report : employee involvement, TQM, and reengineering programs in Fortune 1000 corporations / Edward E. Lawler, with Susan Albers Mohrman, Gerald E. Ledford—1st ed.
        p.   cm.—(Jossey-Bass business & management series)
    Includes bibliographical references (p.   ).
    ISBN 0-7879-4397-5 (alk. paper)
    1. Management—Employee participation—United States. 2. Total quality management—United States. 3. Reengineering (Management)—United States. I. Mohrman, Susan Albers. II. Ledford, Gerald E. III. Title. IV. Series.
    HD660.U5L385   1998
    658.4—dc21   98-8555

FIRST EDITION
PB Printing   10 9 8 7 6 5 4 3 2 1

Contents

Tables
and Figures

Preface

Organizational effectiveness and strategic change are increasingly popular topics in the management literature. Proponents argue that they are the key to gaining a competitive advantage in today's highly competitive business environment. Employee involvement, total quality management, and process reengineering are the most frequently mentioned approaches to improving organizational effectiveness. They also involve complex organizational change processes.

Our interest in employee involvement dates back decades and includes a considerable amount of research and consulting. Despite great interest in the topic and a great deal of research, little systematic information exists on why companies are adopting employee involvement programs, what types of practices they are using, whether there is an increase or decrease in the use of employee involvement, how effective companies think employee involvement is, and how effective it actually is. Much the same is true for total quality management. In many organizations, total quality management is closely related to employee involvement; thus, studying one without the other is ill advised. Reengineering is newer still; as a result, much less research has been done on it. There is little question, however, that it has been widely adopted and that it is controversial in many firms.

Strategies for High Performance Organizations represents the fourth study of a continuing research program aimed at documenting how management practices in Fortune 1000 corporations are changing. The first study involved a 1987 survey that focused on which types of employee involvement practices were being adopted by Fortune 1000 corporations and on the firms' views of the effectiveness of these practices (Lawler, Ledford, and Mohrman, 1989). The second study involved a 1990 follow-up survey of the Fortune 1000 that focused on both employee involvement and total quality management (Lawler, Mohrman, and Ledford, 1992). A comparison of the 1987 and 1990 data showed changes in the adoption rates for employee involvement practices among the large U.S. firms. It also provided a benchmark of the degree to which total quality management practices were actually utilized by U.S. corporations.

The third study collected data in 1993; it provided much more extensive information on who adopts total quality management and employee involvement, as well as on what the results are. In the earlier studies, we considered only the impact of employee involvement and total quality management on nonfinancial performance measures, while the third looked at their effect on such financial results as return on equity.

The information presented here goes beyond the results reported in the first three studies because in this study, in addition to looking at employee involvement and total quality management, we evaluate process reengineering. We also focus for the first time on business and change strategies.

Both managers who are considering changing their management approach and researchers looking for data on how management practices are changing in the United States should find this report useful. Managers who wish to compare their organizational change efforts with others' can use the data to measure their own organizations against those of the Fortune 1000. Managers who are considering changing their organizations should find that the results provide important information about what changes are likely to be effective.

This report begins with a two-section introduction that reviews the past work on organization effectiveness and describes the study. Part One addresses the adoption rate of the major employee involvement practices—namely, those that focus on sharing information, building knowledge, rewarding performance, and sharing power. In each case, we compare the use of these practices in 1987, 1990, 1993, and 1996 and find a selective increase.

Part Two focuses on the adoption of employee involvement, total quality management, and reengineering programs and practices. It begins with an analysis of the patterns by which companies adopt employee involvement practices. Then it looks at the rate of adoption of total quality management and process reengineering practices. For total quality management, we compare the adoption rates from 1990, 1993, and 1996. In the case of process reengineering, we look at the adoption rate in 1996. The final section in Part Two analyzes the degree to which companies adopt employee involvement, total quality management, and reengineering in conjunction with each other.

Part Three focuses on how organizations are changing in three areas. The first is the type of employment relationship or contract that they develop with their employees. The second comprises the new organizational approaches that they are using to improve their performance. The third consists of their change management strategies. These areas, covered here for the first time in our studies, provide an interesting view of how organizations are changing. Our research clearly indicates that there is a "new deal" for employees. It also points out that organizations are doing a variety of things to improve their effectiveness. Finally, the results show that organizational change efforts are often led by senior managers and guided by a clear sense of direction and mission.

Part Four focuses on the effectiveness of employee involvement, total quality management, and reengineering practices and programs. The results are consistently positive for all three of these programs as a whole, as well as for many of the specific practices that they involve. Particularly interesting are the results that show a link between the adoption of employee involvement, total quality management practices, process reengineering, and the financial performance of corporations over time. Finally, the data suggest that the most effective organizational change programs combine employee involvement, total quality management, and reengineering in ways that create a complete organizational change effort.

Part Five focuses on the factors that lead to adoption of employee involvement, total quality management, and reengineering. There are a number of important relationships between the adoption of employee involvement, total quality management, and reengineering change efforts and the characteristics of the organizations and their environments. These relationships suggest that corporations choose all three of these programs because they fit the firm's strategic agenda. The data also suggest that these programs are frequently combined with major structural changes in the way organizations operate.

Acknowledgments. Our study is one focus of the research program of the Center for Effective Organizations. The center, which is part of the Marshall School of Business at the University of Southern California, is sponsored by a number of corporations interested in organizational effectiveness. Their financial support and that of the Marshall School provided the funding for this study. The Sloan Foundation provided financial support that allowed us to do the financial analyses presented in our earlier publications. The Association for Quality and Participation commissioned the 1993 study and provided support for the 1990 survey.

A study like this requires that people in organizations take time to complete the questionnaires that we distributed. We are deeply appreciative of the time spent by members of the Fortune 1000 companies in responding to this survey.

Any research study of this magnitude requires a high level of staff support. We are fortunate at the Center for Effective Organizations to have a talented staff to assist our research activity. We would particularly like to acknowledge the excellent help we received in data collection and data analysis from Alice Yee Mark, Beth Neilson, and Nora Osganian. Lydia Arakaki did an outstanding job of preparing the manuscript. The financial analyses reported in Section Twenty-One are based on work done by K. R. Subramanyam and George Benson.

Los Angeles, California   Edward E. Lawler III
June 1998   Susan Albers Mohrman
                                   Gerald E. Ledford Jr.

The Authors

Edward E. Lawler III is professor of management and organization in the Marshall School of Business at the University of Southern California (USC). He joined USC in 1978; in 1979, he founded and became director of the university's Center for Effective Organizations. He has been honored as a top contributor to the fields of organizational development, organizational behavior, and compensation and is the author of over two hundred articles and twenty-eight books. His most recent books include *Strategic Pay* (Jossey-Bass, 1990), *Employee Involvement and Total Quality Management* (Jossey-Bass, 1992), *The Ultimate Advantage* (Jossey-Bass, 1992), *Organizing for the Future* (Jossey-Bass, 1993), *Creating High Performance Organizations* (Jossey-Bass, 1995), *From the Ground Up: Six Principles for Creating the New Logic Corporation* (Jossey-Bass, 1996), and *Tomorrow's Organization* (Jossey-Bass, 1998).

Susan Albers Mohrman is senior research scientist at the Center for Effective Organizations in the Marshall School of Business at the University of Southern California. She received her Ph.D. degree in organizational behavior from Northwestern University. Her research focuses on management and human resource innovations including employee involvement and total quality management, organizational change, organizational design processes, and team design and the lateral organization. She has researched and consulted with a variety of organizations that are redesigning structures and systems to create high performance. Her books include *Self-Designing Organizations: Learning How to Create High Performance* (1989, with T. G. Cummings), *Designing Team-Based Organizations: New Forms for Knowledge Work* (1995, with S. G. Cohen and A. M. Mohrman Jr.), and *Tomorrow's Organization: Crafting Winning Capabilities in a Dynamic World* (1998, with J. R. Galbraith and E. E. Lawler III; all are Jossey-Bass publications).

Gerald E. Ledford Jr. is research professor at the Center for Effective Organizations in the Marshall School of Business at the University of Southern California. He received his Ph.D. degree in psychology from the University of Michigan. He has conducted research, published, and consulted on a wide variety of approaches to improving organizational effectiveness and employee well-being, including employee involvement, innovative reward systems, organization design, job design, and union-management cooperation. He has published sixty articles and book chapters and is coauthor of five books, including *Large-Scale Organizational Change* (Jossey-Bass, 1989), *Employee Involvement and Total Quality Management* (Jossey-Bass, 1992), and *Creating High Performance Organizations* (Jossey-Bass, 1995). He is an active member of the American Psychological Association, the Academy of Management, and the American Compensation Association.

Introduction

Improving Organizational Performance

Competing views of how organizations can most effectively be managed have characterized the field of management since its inception. Until the 1980s, much of the "action" took place in academic journals and inside corporations, so it was not a highly visible public activity. But during the eighties, the situation changed dramatically. Perhaps the defining event of this change occurred in 1982 when Peters and Waterman published their bestseller, *In Search of Excellence*. Suddenly the debate concerning the best way to manage complex organizations became front-page news in the *Wall Street Journal, Business Week,* the *New York Times,* and virtually every other newspaper and magazine in the country. Management and organizational change also became a major industry as consulting firms began billing companies millions of dollars a year for organizational improvement programs and as tapes, books, and seminars, all of them claiming to have found the key to effective management, proliferated.

Why has major concern with the effectiveness of different management approaches developed? We believe the answer lies in the growing consensus that an effective approach to management offers corporations a powerful competitive advantage (Lawler, 1996; Mohrman, Galbraith, and Lawler, 1998). This consensus is new; prior to the 1980s, most executives, consultants, and researchers agreed that while being a well-managed corporation was helpful, it was not the most powerful way to gain a competitive advantage. Instead of competing by coming up with new management innovations, companies competed on the basis of their ability to execute traditional management practices. They all generally accepted the bureaucratic, hierarchical organization model and varied simply in some of the methods they used and how well they executed them.

When the mass acceptance of the traditional bureaucratic paradigm began to break down in the 1980s, a major competition began among competing paradigms. Unfortunately, this competition has generally lacked good data about what practices are being used and how effective they are. Three paradigms, however, have received the most attention: employee involvement (EI), total quality management (TQM), and process reengineering. All three, perhaps because of their popularity, have been accused of being nothing more than fads. And in truth, like a fad, each has frequently been implemented as the program-of-the-month, with little thought or understanding on the part of implementing companies. All three have been adopted, to at least a limited degree, by a wide range of major U.S. corporations. Our previous studies have documented the increasing acceptance of employee involvement and TQM (Lawler, Mohrman, and Ledford, 1995). But calling these approaches fads does not answer the basic—and very important—question of whether they represent part or all of a new management paradigm that can and should replace the traditional, bureaucratic one, nor does it establish who should use them and how effective they are.

In this section, we will review all three, defining each and describing its potential impact on organizational effectiveness. We will also consider the issues involved in managing the organizational changes that occur when a company adopts one or more of these approaches.

Employee Involvement. There is no single authoritative source or theory that defines employee involvement as a management approach. It has a long history dating back to early research on democratic leadership in work organizations. It includes writings on job design, organizational design, pay systems, and organizational change. The research on democratic leadership that began in the 1930s emphasized the consequences of employee involvement in decision making. It shows that under certain conditions employees are more committed to decisions and that better decisions are made if they are involved.

Another important part of the work on employee involvement concerns work design and its impact on intrinsic motivation and job satisfaction. The research on individual job enrichment, as well as the research on self-managing work teams, forms a critical part of the historical thinking that has led to the development of management approaches stressing employee involvement.

Perhaps the most important overall focus in the work on employee involvement concerns locating decisions at the lowest level in the organization (Lawler, 1986). Employee involvement consistently advocates a bottom-up approach to management. Jobs at the lowest level are thought to be best designed when individuals or teams do a complete part of an organization's work process, such as making an entire product or providing a complete service (Hackman and Oldham, 1980). In addition, this approach argues that the individuals or teams need to be given the power, information, and knowledge they need to work autonomously—that is, independent of management control and direction. The job of management is to prepare the individuals and teams to function in an autonomous manner. Management is an enabler, a culture setter, and a supporter rather than a director of employee action.

Some writings on employee involvement place a strong emphasis on reward systems. They suggest combining participation in decision making and democratic supervision with rewards for skill acquisition and for organizational performance. Gainsharing plans, profit-sharing plans, and employee ownership are important reward system practices associated with employee involvement efforts.

Employee involvement programs lead logically to a flattening of the organization and, in many cases, to the elimination of substantial amounts of staff and support work. Such work is often seen either as moving out of the organization or as being done at lower and lower levels within the organization. Employee involvement programs also stress that a substantial amount of the work done by managers and supervisors is unnecessary because it simply supports a command-and-control approach to management that is not needed when employees are involved in their work and are capable of self-managing.

Organizational change is given a considerable amount of attention in the literature on employee involvement. It stresses bottom-up change, and in most cases, it advocates the retraining of supervisors and the redesigning of work relationships at the first level of the organization as a good start. In many respects, employee involvement does not argue for a continuous improvement approach as much as for discontinuous change; it holds that substantial gains in organizational effectiveness are a result of moving to completely new work structures and new ways of organizing work.

Total Quality Management. Just as with employee involvement, there is no single theoretical formulation for total quality management nor any definitive short list of practices that are always associated with it. It has evolved out of the research and experience of such American quality experts as Deming, Juran, and Crosby and of an important Japanese expert, Ishikawa; their writings, as well as the application of their ideas in many Japanese companies and some American firms, allow us to identify the typical characteristics of most TQM programs.

Total quality management is best viewed as a management philosophy that combines the teachings of Deming and Juran on statistical process control and group problem-solving processes with Japanese values concerning quality and continuous improvement.

The movement started to become popular in Japan during the 1950s as the country tried to recover from World War II. During the 1980s it has become increasingly popular in the United States and Europe, probably as a result of the success of Japanese firms in a number of global markets (Womack, Jones, and Roos, 1990).

The definition of what constitutes quality in an organization's functions and activities is a major focus of TQM. Customer reactions are regarded as the best measure of quality. TQM uses internal customers (for example, employees in other departments) to substitute for external customers in measuring the quality of many of the organization's operations. Focusing on quality is considered a way to gain competitive advantage. TQM advocates often argue that if quality is improved, costs will drop and organizations will respond more quickly and effectively to customer requests.

Total quality management programs usually emphasize the importance of top management acting as the main driver of TQM activities (Deming, 1986). There are many reasons for this, but the most important focuses on the view that TQM is a culture, not just a program. It is a culture in the sense that it tries to change the values of the organization and its employees as well as their behavior in multiple areas. Top management support is necessary to ensure that the right priorities are set and that commitment to the principles of TQM exists throughout the organization.

According to such TQM advocates as Deming, most quality problems in organizations are caused by management and the systems they create. Managers are asked to improve these systems so that they do not produce quality problems, particularly those that are due to functions not properly relating to each other.

Estimates of the proportion of quality problems that can be traced back to worker performance problems range from 25 percent to less than 10 percent. Employees are seen as having good ideas on how to improve quality and as wanting to do a good job. In TQM programs, they are asked to contribute their ideas and are often given responsibility for monitoring quality.

The technologies used to support both quality measurement and quality improvement are highly visible elements of TQM programs. A typical program includes techniques that aid issue identification and problem solving. Most employees are trained in their use. They include statistical process control methods, measures of nonconformance, cost of quality, cause and effect analysis, and various group decision-making methods. These methods typically focus on creating and using accurate production and quality information and on the precise measurement and quantification of problems.

TQM places great emphasis on including all employees in the TQM culture. This is where employee involvement—or as it is usually referred to in the TQM literature, empowerment—comes in. Employees are expected to take responsibility for quality in two important respects: they are expected to call attention to quality problems as they do their normal work, and perhaps more important, they are expected to accept the continuous improvement culture and look for ways that they can do their work better. They are also expected to look for ways in which the overall operation of the organization can be improved. To do this, of course, they need skills and information as well as vehicles that allow them to produce change.

In most TQM programs, quality circles and improvement groups are the major vehicles that allow employees to make suggestions and change work processes. Often they work on problems of lateral coordination and make suggestions about how to improve managerial systems, work methods, and work procedures. In some cases, firms encourage employees to meet in their natural work groups to talk about improved approaches and new work methods. TQM programs usually emphasize work process simplification and codification. The objective is to create a simple work flow that carefully specifies work activities.

Typically, employees receive a substantial amount of quality information and training in TQM programs. In many instances, this represents the first time employees will have received training and valid information about quality. Also new may be the chance to influence the work methods and work procedures that influence quality. The implementation of TQM almost always marks the first time that employees have had a chance to monitor the quality of their own work and to make decisions about its adequacy.

Reengineering. The term *reengineering* and the ideas associated with it burst on the management scene in the early 1990s, thanks to several articles in the *Harvard Business Review* (primarily Hammer, 1990) and a spate of books (including Hammer and Champy, 1993) about its advantages. Very few, if any, management approaches have enjoyed the almost instant popularity of reengineering. Unlike employee involvement and total quality management, reengineering's popularity was primarily driven by a group of consulting firms who offered reengineering programs to major U.S. corporations. The names most associated with the reengineering movement are Michael Hammer and James Champy, both of whom have had long careers as consultants. Although reengineering is not firmly rooted in any particular discipline, its strongest roots are in information technology, and perhaps the most visible academic name associated with the movement is Tom Davenport, whose background is in this field. Many of the change activities involved in reengineering are driven by efforts to improve the utilization of computer systems by large organizations.

During the 1990s, consulting firms, notably Gemini, Index, and Anderson Consulting, signed multimillion-dollar contracts with major corporations to do corporate reengineering. For a while, it appeared that virtually every large U.S. corporation had a major reengineering project going on.

When first articulated, reengineering was primarily about improving the lateral processes of an organization and creating an organizational structure that focuses on processes more than functions; as a result, it is often referred to as *process reengineering*. It soon became associated with employee downsizing and headcount reduction. Downsizing, of course, produces immediate cost reductions and can be a major initial positive change in many corporations. Many large corporations were and still are bloated bureaucracies with too many levels of management and too many managers—particularly middle managers.

Although each reengineering project differs somewhat in its features, most of them share some common elements. The change process is almost always top down, and it focuses on using information technology to improve the lateral processes of an organization. It usually places particular emphasis on reducing the cost and cycle time of routine transactions. Perhaps the most common part of an organization to be reengineered is the order administration area; there information technology can help eliminate the often slow, labor-intensive production-line process through which orders travel before they are executed. After reengineering, individuals or small groups with access to interactive on-line databases are typically able to execute an order quickly and respond intelligently to customer inquiries about where their order is in the production process. They are also able to integrate this with information concerning the state of a customer's account and credit.

Although total quality management programs and employee involvement programs address the issue of too much hierarchy, functional specialization, and overhead, they do it in a very gingerly fashion. They rarely recommend dramatic downsizing and the elimination of layers of management. Instead, they argue that over time, as employee involvement takes hold, fewer managers will be needed and that their numbers should be reduced gradually through attrition rather than through immediate and highly directive action on the part of senior management.

In many respects, employee involvement and total quality management set the stage for the popularity of process reengineering. Many employee involvement programs, particularly those that have utilized self-managing teams, have demonstrated the advantages of organizing for lateral activities, showing how much coordination can be improved when lateral relationships are established. They have also pointed out that teams can be self-managing, making fewer layers of management necessary. TQM programs have done a good job of showing how work can be more customer-focused and how, with good process controls, quality can be dramatically improved, making it much less necessary to have extensive quality control functions and many levels of management. All of this information laid the groundwork for the realization on the part of many senior managers that tremendous reductions in management overhead could be realized if employee involvement and total quality management were used.

The rapid development of low-cost intrafirm computer networks was another major enabler of the process reengineering movement. Since the 1950s, articles have proclaimed that middle management would soon be obsolete because of the capability of computers to link people together and to make people more self-managing (Zuboff, 1988). In virtually every decade since, this prediction has been repeated. Suddenly in the 1990s, the idea that information technology can, in fact, substitute for a substantial number of management layers and of managers started to take on a sense of reality. By linking employees directly to each other and providing them with information and expertise, information technology was able to make certain staff support operations unnecessary. This not only made unnecessary those middle managers whose major role is to coordinate the work of individuals in microscopic jobs or functional silos; it also decreased the need for functional staff support specialists in areas like quality control, human resources management, and order administration and scheduling.

Like total quality management and employee involvement, process reengineering got a tremendous push from the cost competition that global corporations faced in the 1980s and 1990s. It offered to make major corporations much more cost-effective, and it argued that it could speed up an organization's response to customers and to the rapidly changing competitive environment. With all these forces at work, it is hardly surprising that process reengineering became extremely popular and experienced widespread implementation.

Similarities and Differences Among Employee Involvement, Total Quality Management, and Process Reengineering. There are some obvious overlaps among the management principles and practices associated with employee involvement, total quality management, and process reengineering. All see employees taking on additional responsibility, improving and expanding their skills, and receiving more and better information. All emphasize the need for improvements and change in organizational systems and the need for managers to change their behavior and roles dramatically. They also emphasize the importance of culture and the idea that organizations are best viewed as complex, interrelated systems rather than as combinations of independent pieces. They all emphasize the advantages of lateral processes, including the fact that lateral management can make levels of management unnecessary and reduce the need for traditional, control-oriented supervision. Finally, they all call for a change in the employment contract from one that is based on loyalty and seniority to one that is based more on performance and skills.

Figure 1.1 summarizes the major differences among TQM, employee involvement, and reengineering (see also Mohrman, Galbraith, and Lawler, 1998). As this figure shows, they differ in discipline base, age, and the suddenness with which they have impacted the business community. Employee involvement has been around for a long time and has slowly grown in its popularity. TQM is newer and enjoyed a dramatic spurt in its popularity during the 1980s, but its growth was slow compared to the almost overnight popularity of process reengineering during the 1990s.

All three approaches stress the importance of teams, but employee involvement stands out here. Through much of its early history, it focused on the development and utilization of self-managing work teams. Inherent in the idea of self-managing work teams is the concept of lateral process management, which was later to become the cornerstone of the process reengineering approach. Historically, employee involvement change efforts often looked at small processes, like part of a production line, while process reengineering has defined processes much more broadly and much more ambitiously. In fact, it has talked about entirely eliminating certain functions, such as marketing and sales, and building an organization around processes alone. This has happened in some companies; Harley-Davidson, for example, claims to have only two processes—business development and order fulfillment.

	EI	TQM	Process Reengineering
Age	Young adult	Adolescent	Infant
Teams	Self-managing teams	Problem solving work cells	Business process
Feedback	Business, unit performance	Customer feedback, quality levels	Process performance
Disciplinary Base	Social science	Quality engineering	Information technology
Implementation Process	Bottom-up	Top-down	Top-down
Preferred Work Design	Enriched	Simplified, standardized	Mixed
Unique Contributions	Group processes, motivational alignment, employee well-being	Quality emphasis, worker tools (such as STATISTICAL PROCESS CONTROL)	Downsizing, process focus, technological change

Figure 1.1   Contrasts: Three Major Management Approaches.

Note: Based on work by G. Ledford.

Employee involvement, total quality management, and process reengineering favor different organizational designs. Employee involvement tends to favor small business units that are, in effect, minibusinesses. Total quality management, on the other hand, focuses heavily on groups that have clearly established customers and quality levels. Process reengineering tends to think more about how far processes extend and how a total corporation can be organized around them. Thus, reengineering is likely to focus on feedback concerning cycle times for an entire process.

One of the places where total quality management and process reengineering differ most from employee involvement lies in the process for implementing change. Advocates of employee involvement have rather consistently argued that the process used to introduce EI should match the ultimate operating state; thus, they believe the change process itself should be highly participative. Employees are put on teams to redesign their work areas, design gainsharing plans, and so on. Both total quality management and process reengineering have been installed in a much more top-down manner. Both have extensively used outside experts or consultants; these experts, after studying the specific firm, simply tell the organization how the work should be reorganized, install new computer and information systems, and train employees in how to operate within the new organizational structure.

More than total quality management and process reengineering, employee involvement has focused on creating rich, challenging, motivating work. Originally, the focus was on creating individually enriched jobs. An extensive literature developed on what makes a job motivating and how to enrich jobs (see, for example, Hackman and Oldham, 1980). Although individual job enrichment is still popular, our previous research has shown that self-managing teams are increasingly becoming the preferred work design for employee involvement programs (Lawler, Mohrman, and Ledford, 1995). There are a number of reasons for this, including the fact that teams are more likely to make supervision unnecessary and that they can manage lateral relationships in ways that make layers of management unnecessary (Lawler, 1996).

Both total quality management and process reengineering are less clear about their preferred work design. Total quality management talks of simplified, standardized jobs that make possible the use of statistical process control. It also stresses that individuals should be responsible for their own quality, thus moving more power into the hands of the employees. At times, TQM programs seem almost to be a throwback to the days of scientific management and simplified standardized jobs, with the difference that now employees can do some of the monitoring of their own performance. In many respects, process reengineering is similar to total quality management when it comes to work design. Its major emphasis is on integrating lateral processes through the use of information technology. It places little attention on whether and how individuals will be motivated to do the work that results from the intensive use of this technology.

Employee involvement, total quality management, and reengineering have all developed important new technologies and concepts. Since they have such different discipline bases, it is hardly surprising that they have contributed somewhat different technologies and approaches. The behavioral science focus of employee involvement, for example, seems to have led it to focus particularly on tools and approaches that promote the development and motivation of employees. Total quality management, on the other hand, has focused more on tools that improve the reliability of work processes and the quality of the products that they produce. Process reengineering has been particularly powerful in developing organizational designs that fit well with modern information technology.

Strategic Change. Increasingly, the literature on organizational effectiveness argues that reengineering, employee involvement, and total quality management make sense only if they fit the overall business strategy of an organization (Lawler, 1996). In many respects, they can be viewed as approaches that build key organizational capabilities; for example, total quality management practices are intended to build customer focus into the organization, as well as, of course, to improve the quality of products and services. This is likely to have an important bottom-line effect for a corporation only if these capabilities are consistent with an organization's strategy and its overall position in the market. Thus, we need to look at the adoption patterns for these programs in the context of how organizations are changing their business strategy.

The adoption of employee involvement, total quality management, or reengineering represents a major organizational change, and the effectiveness of these programs often depends on how well they are installed. This raises the whole issue of implementation strategy and process and of large-scale organizational change. In our earlier studies, we placed relatively little emphasis on the implementation process that companies use in installing total quality management and employee involvement practices. In this study, we will address this important omission.

There are a number of key change strategies that can be identified as important determinants of how effective an organizational improvement program will be. They include the role played by top management, the degree to which the program is company wide versus business-unit specific, and how long term versus short term its orientation is. Overall, most change theories argue that in order to be effective, a major organizational change program needs careful development and needs to adhere to a well-developed change process (see Nadler and others, 1995; O'Toole, 1995). Among the specifics mentioned are the need for a clear business strategy, a strong reason for change, a clear vision of where the organization is going, strong leadership by top management, broad involvement in defining the nature of the change, and a long-term orientation.

Because the change process may determine the impact of an organizational change, it is important to focus on what practices are adopted by corporations as well as how they are installed and how the overall change process is managed. When this information is combined with information on the effectiveness of EI, TQM, and reengineering programs, it should provide a complete picture of how organizations can be made more effective.

The Study

Any assessment of corporate practices in the areas of employee involvement, total quality management, and reengineering needs to look at the adoption rate for programs and for the practices that are consistent with them. In 1987, we conducted a study of the Fortune 1000 firms in order to determine whether companies had incorporated employee involvement practices into their approach to management (Lawler, Ledford, and Mohrman, 1989). In 1990, we repeated this study and added a series of questions on total quality management (Lawler, Mohrman, and Ledford, 1992). The 1990 study, while showing an increase in employee involvement activities, still indicated that a low percentage of employees in the largest U.S. corporations work in an environment that could be described as high involvement or high performance. On the other hand, the companies surveyed generally reported that they were quite satisfied with the results of their employee involvement activities and that they planned to expand them.

Our third study of the Fortune 1000 was conducted in 1993. It too focused on the adoption of employee involvement and total quality management practices. This study, like the 1990 study, showed an increasing use of employee involvement activities but still indicated that a low percentage of employees in the largest U.S. corporations work in environments that could be described as high involvement or high performance. The study also showed an increasing use of total quality management practices. Analysis of the relationship between the use of employee involvement and total quality management practices and organizational effectiveness showed a significant relationship. The more companies adopted total quality management and employee involvement practices, the better their performance became in a number of areas. Particularly important in the 1993 study was the significant relationship between financial performance and the use of employee involvement and total quality management practices.

Purpose of Study. The present study continues our examination of the degree to which companies are using management practices, policies, and behaviors that are associated with employee involvement and total quality management. In particular, it assesses how much change occurred from 1987 to 1996. For the first time, we look at the adoption of reengineering practices, and we focus on the results of employee involvement, total quality management, and reengineering. We also look at the degree of compatibility among the three approaches, and we examine how the environments that organizations face affect their adoption. The study explores another new area when it identifies organizational policies and practices that are supportive of major organizational change efforts and how they relate to corporate strategies. Finally, it examines the changes that are occurring in the contract between corporations and their employees.

Study Method. The 1987 survey was conducted by the U.S. General Accounting Office (GAO). Michael Dulworth was the GAO project leader. At the inception of the study, the GAO brought together a panel of consultants to offer advice on the study's design. This panel included experts on employee involvement systems from both the federal and the private sectors. A design team, including representatives from the University of Southern California's Center for Effective Organizations (Lawler, Mohrman, and Ledford) and Michael Dulworth from the GAO, developed the employee involvement survey questionnaire and analyzed the data. GAO collected the data.

The 1990 survey was designed and conducted by the Center for Effective Organizations at the University of Southern California; financial support was provided by the Association for Quality and Participation. It used many of the same questions that were asked in the 1987 study. In addition, it asked a series of questions about total quality management programs and practices. These questions were added because of growing interest in TQM programs and their close relationship to employee involvement.

The 1993 survey was a further refinement of the 1990 survey. The most significant changes involved adding questions about total quality management, both because of the increased interest in TQM programs and because of the continued focus on quality as a source of competitive advantage. A few new questions were added regarding employee involvement programs, intended to improve our understanding of organizational patterns around the use and impact of EI activities.

The 1996 survey is similar to the 1993 version but includes some new sections. The new questions focus on reengineering, the employment contract, business strategy, and improvement strategies. A glossary defining the employee involvement terms accompanied all surveys. Resource A contains a copy of the 1996 questionnaire, while Resource B shows the glossary that went with it.

Study Sample. The 1987 survey was sent by the GAO to 934 of the companies listed in the 1986 Fortune 1000 listing of the 500 largest service companies and the 500 largest industrial firms. The actual number of companies surveyed was fewer than 1,000 because of acquisitions and mergers. Responses numbered 476, a 51 percent response rate. The responding organizations employed almost nine million full-time employees.

The Center for Effective Organizations at the University of Southern California sent the 1990 survey to 987 organizations on the 1989 Fortune 1000 list. We received responses from 313 organizations for a response rate of 32 percent. One hundred companies responded to both the 1987 survey and the 1990 survey.

The 1993 survey was sent to 985 companies from the 1992 *Fortune* listing of the 1,000 largest U.S. manufacturing and service companies. Responses were received from 279 companies, a response rate of 28 percent. One hundred and thirty-five companies responded to both the 1990 and the 1993 questionnaires.

The 1996 survey was sent to all 1,000 companies from the *Fortune* listing. Mergers and other changes reduced the potential number of respondents to 994. We received responses from 212 companies for a response rate of 22 percent. Eighty companies responded to both the 1993 and the 1996 surveys.

Our 1990, 1993, and 1996 surveys used many of the same mailing and follow-up procedures that the GAO used in 1987, but we did not obtain as high a response rate. Nevertheless, response rates of 32, 28, and 22 percent are impressive given the large number of surveys being sent to companies today and the length of our questionnaire (fifteen pages for the 1996 survey). The higher response rate to the 1987 survey was probably due in part to its sponsorship by the GAO, a credible government agency. In addition, the "lean" nature of most corporations today creates time pressures that may have contributed to the lower response rates. Fortunately, the response rates are high enough to allow us to make some interesting comparisons among the four surveys, as well as among the different types of companies represented in the 1996 sample.

Although all four surveys were sent to companies in the Fortune 1000 at the time of each study, they were not sent to the same companies each time. The period from 1987 to 1996 saw significant shifts in the makeup of the Fortune 1000; only 650 companies were on both the 1986 and 1992 Fortune 1000 lists, for example. *Fortune* created more change when it dropped the distinction between manufacturing and service firms and simply identified the 1,000 largest firms in 1996. This rate of change in the Fortune 1000 helps account for the fact that we often did not receive responses from the same companies to our 1987, 1990, 1993, and 1996 surveys.

The samples represent a broad array of service and industrial firms. Approximately half of the 1987, 1990, and 1993 samples come from the service sector, and approximately half from the manufacturing sector. The median size of the organizations in the samples is 9,200 in 1987, 10,000 in 1990, 11,000 in 1993, and 14,749 in 1996. The mean distribution of various types of employees in these organizations is almost identical, as the following indicates:

	1987	1990	1993	1996
Hourly/ Clerical:	59 percent	59 percent	54 percent	54 percent
Technical/ Professional:	20 percent	20 percent	24 percent	27 percent
Supervisory/ Managerial:	14 percent	14 percent	15 percent	14 percent
Other:	8 percent	9 percent	6 percent	5 percent

Our conclusion is that the samples appear to be generally comparable. This is an important point, as it means that any differences in results among the surveys are likely to be due to actual changes in how Fortune 1000 companies are managing their business rather than to the fact that different companies responded to the surveys. Where possible, we checked this by comparing the 1987, 1990, 1993, and 1996 survey data for those companies that responded to more than one survey, and we found the results to be generally consistent.

In 45 percent of the cases, responses to the 1996 survey came from managers responsible for human resources. The other 65 percent were completed by a wide variety of senior executives, typically someone in the corporate office two levels below the chief executive officer.

Our data do have important limitations. They address only the 1,000 largest companies in the United States and thus say nothing about what is happening in the many smaller companies that constitute a large and growing part of the U.S. economy. Furthermore, they represent a view from the top. Senior managers completed most of the surveys. The views from other levels in the organizations—from middle managers, front-line supervisors, production workers, and union leaders—may be different.

Despite its limitations, this report is the most comprehensive accounting of practices and approaches to organizational improvement efforts in large corporations that is currently available. No comparable data set exists covering employee involvement and total quality management activities in such a broad array of corporations. Particularly important is the possibility of comparing 1987, 1990, 1993, and 1996 data in order to determine how management approaches and practices are changing. Our data offer a unique opportunity to investigate major corporate change initiatives at various stages of implementation and in a variety of industrial and service organizations.

PART ONE

Employee Involvement: Information, Knowledge, Rewards, and Power

Sharing Information

Basic to employee involvement in organizations is the sharing of information about business performance, plans, goals, and strategies. Without business information, individuals find it hard to understand how the business is doing and to make meaningful contributions to its success: they are not able to participate in planning and setting direction, for example, or to make good suggestions about how products and services can be improved or about how work processes in their area can be accomplished more effectively. Finally, without information, employees cannot alter their behavior in response to changing conditions nor will they have feedback about the effectiveness of their performance and that of the organization.

Thus, the absence of business information limits individuals simply to carrying out prescribed tasks and roles in a relatively automatic bureaucratic way. They are prevented from understanding, participating in, and managing themselves and the business they are part of. For this reason, information is a key building block in most, if not all, organizational improvement efforts that stress the ability of individuals to add value through their participation in the business.

Table 3.1 provides responses to a question on the types of information that are shared. As it shows, most organizations share information about the company's overall operating results with 80 or more percent of their employees. This was true in 1987, 1990, and 1993, and again in 1996. The results also show a continued increase in the sharing of all kinds of information from 1987 to 1996.

Every organization in the study is a public corporation and, by law, must provide financial information to shareholders. At a minimum it seems that organizations would give their employees the same information they give their shareholders in their annual reports. If anything is surprising about the results shown in Table 3.1, it is how many organizations do not share financial results with all employees. Fourteen percent of the companies still do not give most of their employees information about the company's performance, even though this information is public. Further, only 76 percent of the companies give all or almost all their employees information about their overall operating results. This could be accomplished simply by sending an annual report to all employees. The obvious conclusion

Table 3.1	Percentage of Employees Receiving Information.

Information-Sharing Practice		None or Almost None[1] (0–20 percent)	Some (21–40 percent)	About Half (41–60 percent)	Most (61–80 percent)	All or Almost All[1] (81–100 percent)
Corporate Operating Results	1987	6	9	5	13	66
	1990	9	11	4	10	66
	1993	7	7	2	12	73
	1996	3	6	5	11	76
Unit Operating Results	1987	7	20	14	30	30
	1990	11	21	15	20	34
	1993	7	14	13	20	46
	1996	5	11	12	21	51
New Technologies	1987	17	37	21	17	9
	1990	28	35	13	16	9
	1993	17	36	16	15	16
	1996	15	36	17	15	18
Business Plans/Goals	1987	9	24	19	25	23
	1990	12	26	15	22	25
	1993	10	21	15	20	34
	1996	6	19	16	20	38
Competitors' Performance	1987	33	39	14	9	7
	1990	34	31	15	10	10
	1993	27	33	15	11	14
	1996	28	27	17	15	13

[1]For 1990, 1993, and 1996, responses to "None" and "Almost None" were combined and responses to "All" and "Almost All" were combined to convert a seven-point response scale to a five-point response scale.

here seems to be that in a significant number of companies some employees are not treated as important stakeholders in and contributors to the company's performance.

Although important in helping employees view the business as a whole, information about the overall performance of a large company may, for practical purposes, be of limited utility to many employees. The corporate operating results are a considerable distance from their job activities and may not relate directly to what they do. Information on their unit's operating results is likely to be much more meaningful to most employees.

As can be seen from Table 3.1, 72 percent of the companies share data on the performance of their work unit with more than 60 percent of their employees. However, over a third of all companies do not regularly share unit operating results with most employees. The results for 1987, 1990, 1993, and 1996 do show an increase over time in information sharing about business unit results. This is an encouraging trend. However, it will have to continue in order for most employees to receive the kind of information necessary for them to be involved in the business of their organization.

The situation is similar with respect to information sharing about new technologies. Only 33 percent of the corporations say they provide most of their employees with information about new technologies that may affect them. Without this information, employees cannot participate in the planning activities that are involved in the start-up of new technology, nor can they influence decisions about the adoption and acquisition of new technologies. Lack of information concerning new technologies also prevents employees from knowing what skills and knowledge they need to develop.

Only a little over half (59 percent) of companies provide most employees with information on the plans and goals of the business. This is obviously a key information area with respect to employee participation in problem-solving groups, self-managing work teams, and strategy or planning groups.

It is clear from the data in Table 3.1 that the typical employee gets extremely limited feedback on relative business performance. Only 28 percent of the organizations provide data on competitors' performance to most or all employees. This is an important point because it means that most employees cannot make informed judgments about whether their business is winning or losing in the market.

To get an idea of the concentration of information sharing within companies, we counted the number of different kinds of information shared with at least 40 percent of employees. Table 3.2 shows the percent of companies sharing from none to all of the five kinds of information listed in Table 3.1. The data from 1987, 1990, 1993 and 1996 are similar. The 1996 data show that 54 percent of companies share four or more of the five kinds of information with at least 40 percent of employees, and 28 percent share all kinds. This means that in 1996 a few more companies were broadly providing information than was true in 1993, and it reinforces the indication of a trend among organizations toward sharing more kinds of information with their employees.

Do employee involvement programs increase the information flow in organizations? As shown in Figure 3.1, the answer appears to be yes. The most common response to this question in 1987, 1990, 1993, and 1996—that involvement activities increase information flow to a moderate degree—was to be expected, since information is so critical to all aspects of involvement. If anything is surprising, it is that the responses to this question are not more positive.

Overall, our results show that Fortune 1000 corporations still share only limited information with their employees. As a general rule, the further information gets from the results of the total corporation, the less likely it is that employees are given the information. This is

Table 3.2	Percentage of Companies Sharing Information with More Than 40 Percent of Employees.			
Number of Kinds of Information Shared	1987 ($n = 323$)	1990 ($n = 313$)	1993 ($n = 279$)	1996 ($n = 212$)
0	6	8	6	3
1	11	15	11	7
2	19	21	14	16
3	22	17	20	20
4	26	23	24	26
5	16	16	25	28

Five possible kinds: company's overall operating results, unit operating results, advance information on new technology, business plans/goals, competitors' relative performance.

understandable in one respect: in many cases, organizations are not required to distribute information about how a business unit is doing or about new technologies to their employees or the public. However, not distributing this information to employees may have significant costs associated with it and may be a major obstacle to any organizational improvement efforts.

The typical employee in companies that do not share information may not understand how well the business is doing and is likely to have little sense of what it must do to be competitive. Information about the performance of business units is often the most important information for employees to have if they are to be involved in a business for which they have a "line of sight" with respect to the impact of their behavior. Awareness of corporate results helps employees understand the larger business context, but it is at the unit level where most of them can make a difference and can relate to performance results. Information at this level is also what they need in order to contribute ideas and suggestions and be involved in the business.

There is change from 1987 to 1996, but not the amount of change that might be expected given the critical importance of information

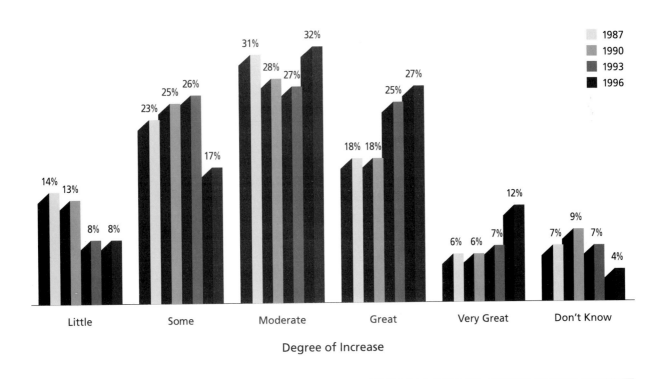

Figure 3.1   Percentage of Companies Indicating Degree to Which Information Has Increased as a Result of Employee Involvement.

to many employee involvement and total quality management programs. In essence, many organizations provide only what the law requires them to make available to shareholders: overall business results. Most employees do not get good information on the direction and success of the business. Given this, we find it hard to imagine employees being meaningfully involved in decisions concerning the business of which they are a part. They are also not likely to be in a position to make informed decisions about their own development and careers.

SECTION 4

Knowledge Development

Organizational effectiveness increasingly depends on the skills and knowledge of the workforce. Without the right skills, individuals cannot do their jobs effectively, much less participate in a business and influence its direction, as EI programs advocate. To be successful, total quality management programs demand that employees acquire a variety of skills. And since reengineering programs often lead to work that is more laterally integrated and based on information technology, they too require that employees learn new skills.

Table 4.1 reports on the prevalence of training for some of the skills frequently identified as necessary for effective employee involvement, total quality management, and reengineering (Commission on the Skills of the American Workforce, 1990). Three of these skills are essentially interpersonal and group skills. We have included them because so many EI and TQM processes involve meetings, interpersonal interactions, group problem solving, and the ability to influence others. The two technical skills, quality and statistical analysis and business understanding, are included because they are central to most organizational improvement and total quality management efforts. Finally, we also asked about job-skills training (1990, 1993, and 1996 only) and about cross-training.

The results for training in group decision-making and problem-solving skills show a general increase from 1987 to 1996. Despite this increase, the 1996 results still show less than a majority of employees receiving training in these skills. The increase from 1990 to 1993 is particularly impressive. Little change, however, occurred from 1993 to 1996, suggesting that the growth in training in this area has plateaued.

The results for leadership training show a general increase from 1987 to 1996. Even with the increase, however, only a small percentage of

Table 4.1 **Percentage of Employees Receiving Training in the Past Three Years.**

		None or Almost None[1] (0–20 percent)	Some (21–40 percent)	About Half (41–60 percent)	Most (61–80 percent)	All or Almost All[1] (81–100 percent)
Group Decision-Making/ Problem-Solving Skills	1987	41	43	11	4	1
	1990	45	37	12	5	1
	1993	28	42	15	11	5
	1996	28	37	18	9	8
Leadership Skills	1987	37	51	10	2	1
	1990	46	42	8	2	1
	1993	33	45	14	4	3
	1996	31	42	16	8	3
Skills in Understanding Business	1987	48	39	8	4	1
	1990	61	34	4	2	0
	1993	59	33	4	4	1
	1996	39	40	12	6	3
Quality/Statistical Analysis Skills	1987	58	28	7	6	1
	1990	57	25	10	5	3
	1993	38	28	12	13	10
	1996	45	22	15	9	9
Team-Building Skills	1987	45	36	13	4	1
	1990	44	34	14	6	1
	1993	26	36	21	9	9
	1996	21	33	23	14	8
Job-Skills Training	1987	—	—	—	—	—
	1990	16	28	21	20	14
	1993	11	18	22	27	22
	1996	7	20	23	26	24
Cross-Training	1987	35	36	16	9	4
	1990	32	41	17	7	3
	1993	31	41	15	9	4
	1996	34	33	18	10	5

[1]For 1990, 1993, and 1996, responses to "None" and "Almost None" were combined and responses to "All" and "Almost All" were combined to convert a seven-point response scale to a five-point response scale.

the companies trained more than 60 percent of their workforce in leadership skills. Indeed, only 27 percent trained more than 40 percent of their employees. In a traditional organization, this is to be expected, since hierarchical organizations see leadership as resting with a few employees at the top of the organization; thus, training a large number of leaders is not cost-effective. In an organization that is encouraging individuals throughout the organization to take a role in its management, quite the opposite is true. Individuals throughout the firm need to lead teams, manage projects, and generally provide a sense of direction for the corporation (Mohrman, Cohen, and Mohrman, 1995; Lawler, 1996). It follows logically that leadership training should be broadly spread throughout the organization and not be the exclusive purview of a small group of senior managers (Tichy, 1997).

The results for training individuals in the skills necessary to understand how businesses operate show a significant increase. This increase is particularly noticeable from 1993 to 1996, but overall the evidence clearly indicates that in the majority of corporations, most employees do not receive training in understanding business. The relatively low level of training in this area can be a significant problem in businesses that wish to increase employee involvement. Clearly understanding the performance measures and operations of the business requires good financial skills. Without them, individuals will have a hard time participating knowledgeably in problem-solving groups, much less operating effectively in self-managing work teams or understanding a profit-sharing or stock option plan. Basic business literacy is a precondition for almost any organizational improvement effort.

As can be seen from the table, most employees were not trained during the three years prior to 1996 in the quality and statistical skills necessary for an employee involvement or total quality management program to work effectively (Deming, 1986; Juran, 1989). However, the results do differ from those obtained in 1987 and 1990. Perhaps because of the national focus on total quality management and statistical analysis, there was a definite increase in 1993 in the training of employees in quality skills. The 1996 data show no further increase but remain at a level higher than those of 1987 and 1990.

Although there was an encouraging increase in training for team-building skills from 1990 to 1993, there was no increase from 1993 to 1996. Most individuals still are not being trained in the team and interpersonal skills needed for them to participate in problem-solving groups and team-based decision making.

The data are more positive with respect to job skills; 50 percent of the companies surveyed provide training to most of their employees. This is a significant increase from 1990 (34 percent). Fifteen percent cross-trained a majority of their employees, representing little change from earlier years.

Although the trend with respect to training is encouraging, these levels stand in notable contrast to the policies of such exemplary companies as Motorola, which mandates one week's training for all employees each year (see Wiggenhorn, 1990). One interesting trend is apparent from the results reported in Table 4.1. With one exception, there has been a decline in companies saying only a few individuals get a particular kind of training, while there is a noticeable increase in the number of companies reporting that most of their workforce gets a particular kind of training. In other words, the extremes of the distribution seem to have changed significantly, perhaps reflecting the belief on the part of some leading companies that everyone must receive a particular kind of training if that training is to be taken seriously. The one exception to this general statement seems to be in the area of cross-training, where little change is apparent.

What accounts for the poor, if improving, record of most corporations in the area of training? One possibility is that the window of time we asked about is too small. We asked about training only in the prior three years; it may be that many organizations trained their employees earlier. Unfortunately, there is no way of knowing whether this is true. It is true that in some areas, individuals may not need to be trained every three years. Thus, looking only at a three-year training window could underestimate the percentage of employees in corporations that are actually trained in areas like understanding business results and statistical process control.

The actual number who have been trained in a company at any point in time is undoubtedly larger than the number that have been trained in the last three years. Nevertheless, a strong case can be made that individuals need to be regularly trained in most of the areas we studied. With the rate of change in many organizations, old training often amounts to no training. Work methods, technologies, and business systems now change at such a rapid rate that constant updating of the important skills in these areas is necessary in order for individuals to operate effectively. Data from a variety of international comparative studies confirm that U.S. manufacturing companies are relatively low spenders on training and need to do more training (see, for example, Kochan and Osterman, 1994; Pfeffer, 1994).

A count of how many types of training each company provides is shown in Table 4.2. It shows that in the three years prior to 1996, only 7 percent of the responding companies trained 40 percent or more of their employees in all five of these areas. This is a small increase from the 3 percent who did this amount of training in 1993. Thirty-five percent did not train 40 percent or more in any of the areas, a significant decrease from 1993 (44 percent) and a large decrease from 1987 when 63 percent didn't train 40 percent or more of their employees in any of these areas.

The results change significantly when job skills are included as a kind of training (see Table 4.3). Here only 15 percent of the companies provided no training in any of these areas to 40 percent or more of their employees. This represents a small change from 1993 but a big change from the 1990 results. It clearly indicates that more training is being done.

Do employee involvement programs lead to more training and skill development? The data in Figure 4.1 suggest that the answer is yes. Most companies indicate that involvement has led to some or a moderate increase in skill development.

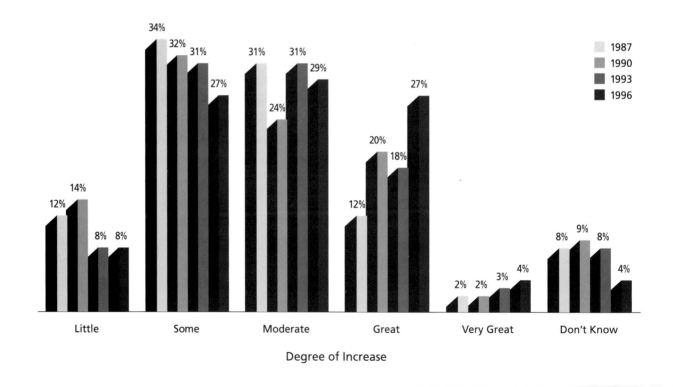

Figure 4.1   Percentage of Companies Indicating Degree to Which Skill Development Increased as a Result of Employee Involvement.

Table 4.2	Percentage of Companies Providing Five Kinds of Training to More Than 40 Percent of Employees in the Past Three Years.

Number of Kinds of Training Shared	1987 (n = 323)	1990 (n = 313)	1993 (n = 279)	1996 (n = 212)
0	63	59	44	35
1	16	22	15	17
2	12	8	19	20
3	6	7	11	15
4	2	2	7	6
5	1	1	3	7

Five possible kinds: group decision making/problem solving, leadership, business understanding (accounting and so on), quality/statistical analysis, team building.

Table 4.3	Percentage of Companies Providing Six Kinds of Training to More Than 40 Percent of Employees in the Past Three Years.

Number of Kinds of Training Provided	1990 (n = 313)	1993 (n = 279)	1996 (n = 212)
0	34	20	15
1	32	28	25
2	19	14	15
3	6	19	19
4	6	10	15
5	2	6	6
6	1	3	6

Six possible kinds: group decision making/problem solving, leadership, business understanding (accounting and so on), quality/statistical analysis, team building, job-skills training.

Overall, the data suggest an improving situation with respect to the training of employees in U.S. corporations. Most major U.S. corporations apparently are making greater investments in training. This is encouraging given the many studies that have found that the American workforce is poorly prepared to face global competition (Dertouzos, Lester, and Solow, 1989; Reich, 1991).

Although training is growing, it most likely still falls short of the level needed for employees to keep up with the technological changes that are occurring and for employee involvement and total quality management to work—indeed, for most businesses to perform effectively, regardless of what management approach they use. The lack of training certainly means that many employees do not have the necessary skills to become full business partners. A small but growing number of companies are the exception, making major commitments to training most of their employees in the skills needed to have successful TQM and EI programs.

SECTION 5

Rewards

Reward systems can play an important role in determining the success or failure of any organizational improvement effort because they can be a key driver of behavior. In order to support employment involvement, reward systems need to be designed in a way that supports individuals obtaining more information about the business, adding to their skills, and taking on more decision-making responsibility (Lawler, 1990). Two features of reward systems are particularly important. The first involves the degree to which pay is based on performance. When pay is based on performance, it has the potential to motivate improved performance. Two elements of pay-for-performance systems determine whether they do, in fact, motivate behavior that supports involvement and organizational effectiveness: the first is the kind of performance that is measured, and the second is the amount of money that depends on performance. In order for pay to be a motivator, a significant amount must be tied to measures of performance that are easy to understand and capable of being influenced.

The second feature of reward systems that is crucial for employee involvement concerns how the base pay of individuals is structured and set. In order for a pay system to support EI, it needs to send the proper messages about individual development, growth, learning, and the culture of the organization.

Basing rewards on organizational performance is one way to encourage employees to be involved in and care about the performance of their company (Lawler, 1990). It also helps ensure that they share in the gains that result from any performance improvement. Table 5.1 shows the popularity of four approaches to basing cash payments on performance. It also presents information on the popularity of stock and recognition reward programs.

Individual incentive plans are usually not very supportive of employee involvement, total quality management, or reengineering. They focus on individuals' performance and do not tie the individual into the overall success of the business; moreover, they can interfere with teamwork, group problem solving, a process focus, and lateral integration (Schuster and Zingheim, 1992). In situations where individuals hold jobs that can be done independently of others, individual incentive plans may be quite functional. They can motivate individuals to take charge of their particular area of responsibility and perform effectively. The pattern for individual incentives shown in Table 5.1 is interesting. All but 9 percent of the corporations report having some employees covered by individual incentives; however, these systems typically cover 20 percent or less of the workforce. A comparison between 1993 and 1996 shows a slight increase in the use of individual incentive plans.

Team incentives can be supportive of employee involvement activities such as work teams and problem-solving groups. They can also be supportive of reengineering efforts that focus on creating process teams and lateral integration. The results show that they are increasingly popular. Eighty-seven percent of the companies surveyed use them. The increase in their use matches the increasing use of teams, which will be discussed in the next section. When used these incentives still tend to cover small numbers of employees (less than 21 percent). This finding makes sense, as many individuals do not work in teams or teamwork situations. Further, many U.S. employees prefer to be paid for their individual performance.

Profit sharing, stock ownership, stock options, and gainsharing are approaches that can link employees more closely to the success of the business and reward them for it. These systems are often cited as the reward approaches most supportive of employee involvement (Blinder, 1990; Lawler, 1992; Schuster and Zingheim, 1992). The results show that profit sharing and employee stock ownership are the most widely used and the most likely to be available to most or all employees.

		None (0 percent)	Almost None (1–20 percent)	Some (21–40 percent)	About Half (41–60 percent)	Most (61–80 percent)	Almost All (81–99 percent)	All (100 percent)
Individual Incentives	1987	13	49	27	6	2	1	2
	1990	10	46	24	8	5	3	5
	1993	10	40	30	8	3	4	5
	1996	9	34	27	9	7	6	8
Work-Group or Team Incentives	1990	41	38	10	6	1	2	3
	1993	30	40	14	6	3	3	5
	1996	13	45	21	8	2	4	6
Gainsharing	1987	74	19	4	1	0	1	1
	1990	61	28	8	1	1	1	0
	1993	58	26	7	2	3	2	2
	1996	55	26	9	3	1	2	4
Profit Sharing	1987	35	20	11	4	5	10	15
	1990	37	19	7	4	6	10	17
	1993	34	23	7	4	3	11	19
	1996	31	18	7	3	9	13	20
Employee Stock Ownership Plan	1987	39	8	4	4	6	10	28
	1990	36	9	6	3	5	13	29
	1993	29	9	9	4	6	14	30
	1996	32	9	4	3	5	15	32
Stock Option Plan	1993	15	56	15	2	1	2	10
	1996	13	46	21	2	3	5	10
Nonmonetary Recognition Awards for Performance	1990	9	23	18	10	13	10	17
	1993	6	22	17	7	10	17	22
	1996	4	17	17	10	16	12	25

Note: Not all questions were asked in 1987 and 1990.

Historically, gainsharing is the approach that has been most closely identified with employee involvement since it stresses involvement as a key to the success of its financial bonus system. As Table 5.1 shows, gainsharing is clearly the least popular approach. Fifty-five percent of responding companies say none of their employees are covered by a gainsharing plan. Of the corporations that offer some employees gainsharing, virtually all have a minority of their total workforce on it. Rare (only 4 percent of companies that responded in 1996) is the corporation that covers all employees with gainsharing.

A comparison between the 1987 and 1990 results shows a significant increase in the use of gainsharing; however, the growth was slower from 1990 to 1996. This is somewhat surprising given the earlier growth. One possible explanation is that gainsharing plans have already been installed in a significant percentage of the situations where they fit well. Future growth may depend on the development of new approaches to gainsharing that make these plans applicable to new settings.

Twenty percent of the companies cover all employees with profit sharing, while 69 percent have a profit-sharing plan. Given its problems as a motivator (a poor line of sight from behavior to reward in large companies) and its use rate, we think it's safe to conclude that profit sharing is not acting as an important motivator of involvement or performance in most companies. The results from 1987 to 1996 show no significant increase in the use of profit sharing despite an increasing emphasis in the management literature on the use of variable or bonus-based pay (Blinder, 1990; Schuster and Zingheim, 1992; Lawler, 1996).

Reward systems that use stock are generally consistent with employee involvement because they can help create an ownership mentality or culture. As is true with profit sharing, however, they are likely to have a poor line of sight and thus are not very effective motivators of performance in large organizations. Stock ownership plans are available to all employees in 32 percent of the corporations surveyed. It is likely that this result reflects the widespread use of employee stock purchase plans (Blasi, 1988; Rosen, Klein, and Young, 1986). In 32 percent of the corporations surveyed, stock ownership plans are not available to any employees. It is one of the few practices that companies tend to offer to all or none of their employees. Somewhat surprisingly, there is little evidence of an increase in their popularity from 1987 to 1996.

The results for stock option plans show that in most companies they cover only a small percentage of the employees—probably the senior managers. During 1997, the implementation of company-wide stock option plans by Pepsico, Bank of America, and other large companies sparked considerable interest in such programs, so there is reason to believe that all-employee stock option plans are becoming more popular. Our results, however, suggest little growth from 1993 to 1996.

The actual frequency of reward activities oriented toward employee involvement may be a bit inflated in Table 5.1 because profit-sharing, stock option, and employee stock ownership plans (ESOPs) are included. Many profit-sharing plans have been around for years and are often best thought of as retirement benefits rather than incentives. Many ESOPs have been installed for tax advantages and are not tied to employee involvement (Blasi, 1988). We might also question the effectiveness of profit-sharing plans and ESOPs because they have a poor line of sight. In addition, the general lack of information and knowledge about the business that exists in many companies reduces the line of sight even more. Without information and knowledge, variable rewards often appear capricious, rather than motivating and involving.

Companies sometimes use nonmonetary recognition programs to support employee involvement efforts. These reward systems are also frequently advocated by proponents of TQM programs. Table 5.1 shows that most organizations have recognition programs, but they cover all employees in only 25 percent of the firms. This suggests that they are typically targeted at special activities and groups. The data do show a little growth in their popularity from 1990 to 1996; this may well reflect their increasing use as part of total quality management programs.

Figure 5.1 suggests that the responding companies feel employee involvement has had a limited effect on the degree to which performance-based rewards have increased at lower levels. The 1996, 1993, 1990, and 1987 data show similar results. In fact, according to our respondents, employee involvement has had less of an effect on rewards than it has had on information sharing and knowledge.

Table 5.2 shows the concentration of the five pay-for-performance reward system approaches. Only 18 percent of companies are using none of them widely. A majority of these companies use at least two of these reward practices. This reflects a significant increase from 1990 and a continuation of the trend that was apparent in 1993. Despite the increased use of pay for performance, the opportunity still exists for many organizations to reward many more individuals for their performance.

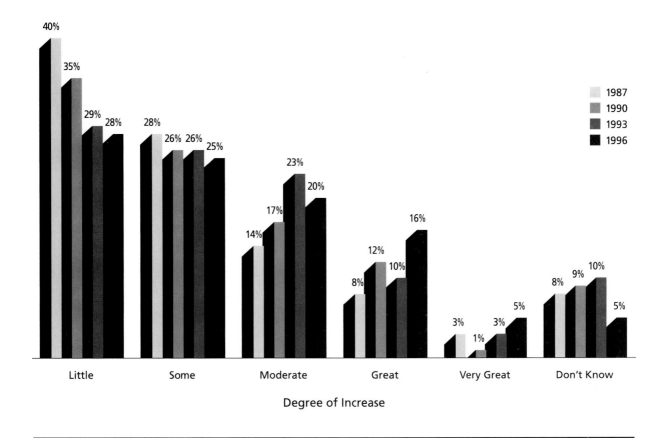

Figure 5.1   Percentage of Companies Indicating Degree to Which Performance-Based Rewards at Lower Levels Increased as a Result of Employee Involvement.

Table 5.3 presents the results for five additional reward system practices that are considered supportive of employee involvement. The first of these practices, all-salaried pay, reduces the distinctions between exempt and nonexempt employees, thus creating a pay system more congruent with the notion of an egalitarian workforce. The table shows that over two-thirds of companies use this approach. A comparison between 1993 and 1996 shows no significant change in the use of all-salaried workforces.

When pay is based on knowledge and skill, it rewards individuals for their capability and flexibility in contributing to the organization. As a person learns more and can contribute more to the organization, his or her pay increases (Ledford, 1991). This approach fosters and rewards cross-training and makes possible the flexible deployment of people. It can also be supportive of teaming and encouraging individuals to learn skills needed for their involvement in the business. Finally, it can promote a broader understanding of how the business operates, which can be useful in addressing complex problems. Table 5.3 shows that 62 percent of companies use this approach, although most with only a minority (1 to 20 percent) of their workforce.

Table 5.2	Percentage of Companies Using Performance-Based Reward Practices with More Than 40 Percent of Employees.		
Number of Kinds of Reward Practices	1990 ($n = 313$)	1993 ($n = 279$)	1996 ($n = 212$)
0	29	24	18
1	38	41	30
2	24	21	32
3	8	8	16
4	2	5	3
5	0	1	1

Five possible kinds: individual incentives, profit sharing, gainsharing, employee stock ownership, work-group or team incentives.

A comparison among the 1987, 1990, 1993, and 1996 data shows significant growth in the use of skill-based pay. The number of companies employing it has increased from 40 to 62 percent. The growth, however, slowed from 1993 to 1996, and it is not clear why. One possibility is that this practice reached a saturation point. It seems to fit best in manufacturing and service situations where first-level employees are cross-trained, and there are only so many of these situations. It may also be encountering significant resistance. Skill-based pay, after all, is not an easily added "extra"; it represents a major change in the way an organization determines base pay. Many base pay systems have been in place for decades and are not easily altered; they must be changed in a major way if skill-based pay is adopted.

There does seem to be increased interest in competence-based pay (Mohrman, Galbraith, and Lawler, 1998). Like skill-based pay, it focuses on paying the person, not the job, but it is usually applied to managers and knowledge workers. Its use was not measured in our survey. A good guess is that if it had been, we would have found more growth in the trend of paying the person instead of paying the job.

Flexible benefits programs provide employees with some control over how the benefit portion of their compensation package is structured. This approach fits with the employee involvement philosophy of moving responsibility for decisions to those individuals who are

Table 5.3 **Percentage of Employees Covered by EI-Supportive Reward Practices.**

		None (0 percent)	Almost None (1–20 percent)	Some (21–40 percent)	About Half (41–60 percent)	Most (61–80 percent)	Almost All (81–99 percent)	All (100 percent)
All-Salaried Pay Systems	1987	29	15	13	10	12	11	10
	1990	36	18	14	10	7	9	7
	1993	27	18	11	13	11	11	9
	1996	30	14	18	13	12	8	6
Knowledge/ Skill-Based Pay	1987	60	25	7	2	2	2	2
	1990	49	34	11	2	1	1	1
	1993	40	37	12	4	2	2	3
	1996	38	40	13	2	4	1	2
Flexible, Cafeteria-Style Benefits	1987	66	7	4	3	2	6	13
	1990	46	12	5	4	5	9	20
	1993	32	9	7	4	7	12	30
	1996	32	7	6	5	5	11	33
Employment Security	1987	47	14	6	2	6	8	18
	1990	47	20	6	4	6	9	8
	1993	63	13	5	2	3	5	9
	1996	65	15	4	3	5	3	6
Open Pay Information	1993	34	17	8	7	6	9	20
	1996	30	18	6	7	8	10	21

affected by them. Sixty-eight percent of companies used flexible benefits in 1996. Flexible benefits increased tremendously in their popularity from 1987 to 1993 but showed little growth from 1993 to 1996. Although flexible benefits programs fit with employee involvement because of their emphasis on employee choice in the reward mix, the increased adoption of this approach may have more to do with controlling benefit costs and meeting the needs of an increasingly diverse workforce than with supporting involvement. The cost of benefits, particularly health care, has been increasing dramatically, and many companies are using flexible benefits and cost sharing as ways to control these costs (Lawler, 1990).

The results concerning employment security are interesting. Some recent books and articles on organizational effectiveness argue that employment security is an important enabler of involvement and total quality management (see, for example, Pfeffer, 1994). Without job security, employees may fear that any improvement they make will threaten their jobs and those of others. As a result, individuals may feel hesitant to get involved in improvement activities. The results show a significant decline from 1987 to 1993 in the number of companies with employment security. Most noticeable is the increase of companies covering no employees with job security from 47 percent of the companies covering no employees to 65 percent. The results for 1996 suggest that the decline in employment security may be over as the 1996 and 1993 results are essentially the same. Perhaps this is because companies have now reached a much lower level of employment, which fits their current business realities. We may, in effect, be seeing the development of employment security models that work on different levels: a high level of job security for "core employees" and a lower one for the rest.

Open pay information is one way to ensure that employees understand how they are paid, a necessary precondition to their participation in decisions about their pay and that of other employees. The results concerning openness show no significant change from 1993 to 1996. They continue to show an interesting split among companies: 21 percent supply all employees with open information while 30 percent supply none. Clearly, companies are operating with two quite different philosophies with respect to providing information about pay.

Overall, the data suggest that organizations are continuing to change their reward system practices. Particularly significant is the finding that organizations are slowly increasing their use of certain pay-for-performance approaches, a change that is potentially quite supportive of employee involvement. It may not have a powerful effect on motivation because some of the approaches, primarily stock and profit sharing, have a poor line of sight. However, it can contribute to employees seeing themselves as having a direct stake in organizational performance.

Moving decision-making power downward in organizations is the core of what employee involvement is all about. It also plays an important role in total quality management programs, since they emphasize empowerment. In order to get a sense of how active organizations have been in moving decision making to lower levels, the survey asked about the existence of a number of specific structural approaches to giving employees more decision-making power. These approaches can be divided into two basic types: parallel structures and work design.

The first type involves special meetings or problem-solving activities that are separate from the normal day-to-day work processes; as a result, they are often referred to as parallel organizational structures (Lawler and Mohrman, 1985; Lawler, 1992). Although problem-solving activities do move some power downward, they are limited in their impact (Ledford, Lawler, and Mohrman, 1988). Typically employees only provide input and recommendations; they do not make substantial decisions, nor do they have the budget or power to implement decisions.

As can be seen in Table 6.1, almost every organization uses some form of parallel structure, and many use more than one. However, the use of all parallel structures is limited to fewer than half of the employees in most organizations that use them.

The trend from 1987 to 1996 shows an increase in the use of employee participation groups. This increase is significant and provides a contrast to the lack of change in the use of quality circles. Apparently companies are adopting employee participation groups instead of expanding their use of quality circles. Quality circles are used in 60 percent of all companies, a percentage that has been essentially stable since 1987. Other types of participation groups are used by 94 percent of all companies, up from 70 percent in 1987.

Union-management quality-of-work-life committees have been tried in a much smaller percentage of the companies. This finding, of course, follows from the relatively low level of union membership in the United States in general and in the surveyed companies in particular (less than 50 percent have union members). Although a comparison between 1987 and 1990 shows a 5 percent increase in the percentage of companies using this approach, a comparison among 1990, 1993, and 1996 shows no significant change. Like quality circles, their use appears to be stable.

| Table 6.1 | | Percentage of Employees Covered by Parallel-Structure Practices. | | | | | | |

		None (0 percent)	Almost None (1–20 percent)	Some (21–40 percent)	About Half (41–60 percent)	Most (61–80 percent)	Almost All (81–99 percent)	All (100 percent)
Quality Circles	1987	39	32	18	7	2	0	1
	1990	34	36	19	7	4	1	1
	1993	35	32	19	6	5	3	1
	1996	40	28	20	6	3	1	2
Employee Participation Groups Other Than QCs	1987	30	33	21	9	3	2	1
	1990	14	35	30	11	5	3	3
	1993	9	26	31	14	13	5	3
	1996	6	28	28	17	9	7	5
Union-Management Quality-of-Work-Life Committees	1987	70	20	7	2	1	1	0
	1990	65	23	9	2	0	0	1
	1993	65	22	6	3	2	2	1
	1996	64	23	9	2	2	0	0
Survey Feedback	1987	32	22	17	6	7	6	10
	1990	23	26	20	5	4	7	16
	1993	15	19	15	8	9	10	25
	1996	9	15	15	8	8	20	26
Suggestion Systems	1987	17	17	16	7	11	11	21
	1990	14	24	14	7	10	12	19
	1993	15	26	19	11	7	9	14
	1996	11	29	23	7	9	7	15

Survey feedback is an activity that does not necessarily entail the creation of a parallel structure, since it often takes place in established work groups. However, it is often seen as an "extra," or special activity. As can be seen in Table 6.1, 91 percent of companies use it for at least some employees. Survey feedback shows a significant increase in popularity from 1987 to 1996.

Finally, our survey asked about the use of suggestion systems. Typically these involve one or more employees submitting a written improvement suggestion. In 1996, 89 percent of the companies reported using them; their rate of use was essentially unchanged from 1987 to 1996. Thus, although they are one of the oldest and perhaps least powerful approaches, suggestion systems continue to be popular and show no sign of becoming less so.

Table 6.2 looks at the prevalence of programs that use work design practices to move power downward. Job enrichment, self-managed work teams, and minibusiness units (defined as partially autonomous small business–like units) all involve a substantial change in the basic structure of the organization and are aimed at moving important operating decisions into the hands of individuals and teams performing basic manufacturing or service work. Finally, employee committees are a way to give employees more say in policy and strategy decisions.

As shown in Table 6.2, job enrichment is used widely and has gained popularity since 1987. The broad acceptance of job enrichment probably results from the fact that this approach has been around for decades and has been widely publicized (see, for example, Herzberg, 1966; Hackman and Oldham, 1980). For the first time, the 1996 results show that job enrichment programs typically affect more than 20 percent of the employees in the organizations where they have been adopted. The historically low coverage rate of these programs may reflect the fact that the literature concerning them has focused on their use for routine assembly and clerical jobs.

The popularity of self-managing work teams and minibusiness units continues to increase. However, they are still used much less frequently than job enrichment. Self-managing work teams are used in 78 percent of the corporations, but in most they involve only a small percentage of the workforce. A comparison of the 1987 and 1990 data shows a significant increase from 28 percent to 47 percent in the use of self-managing work teams; a comparison between 1990 and 1993 shows a further significant increase from 47 percent to 68 percent; and finally, a comparison between 1993 and 1996

Table 6.2	Percentage of Employees Covered by Work Design Power-Sharing Practices.						
		None (0 percent)	Almost None (1–20 percent)	Some (21–40 percent)	About Half (41–60 percent)	Most (61–80 percent)	Almost All (81–99 percent)	All (100 percent)
Job Enrichment or Redesign	1987	40	38	12	6	2	2	1
	1990	25	43	23	6	2	0	1
	1993	18	40	25	8	4	3	3
	1996	13	31	31	14	8	1	2
Self-Managing Work Teams	1987	72	20	6	1	0	0	0
	1990	53	37	9	1	0	0	0
	1993	32	49	15	3	2	0	0
	1996	22	46	23	4	3	2	0
Minibusiness Units	1987	75	18	4	1	1	0	0
	1990	72	23	3	1	0	1	0
	1993	56	23	14	3	4	1	0
	1996	40	35	14	5	4	2	1
Employee Committees Concerned with Policy and/or Strategy	1993	35	45	13	5	2	1	0
	1996	26	50	19	3	1	1	0

Note: Not all questions were asked in 1987 and 1990.

shows an increase from 68 percent to 78 percent. Overall, this reveals a clear pattern of significant continuing growth.

Even though most companies don't have a large number of employees working in teams, these increases are impressive. Installing teams involves much more than creating a temporary parallel structure. In many cases, equipment must be moved, employees trained, supervisors trained and reassigned, and a host of other changes made. Despite these difficulties, the significant changes indicate that work teams are an increasingly popular approach to organizing in the Fortune 1000 companies and that, as a result, real increases in power sharing probably are occurring.

Minibusiness units are used less frequently than any of the other power-sharing practices, and like the others, they tend to affect a small percentage of the organization's employees. Nevertheless, the results show a significant increase in the use of minibusiness units from 1990 to 1993 and from 1993 to 1996. This finding is not surprising given the increase in other power-sharing approaches, particularly teams. This approach involves more power sharing and change than do self-managing teams (Mills, 1991; Lawler, 1996). The increased popularity of minibusiness units may mean that a growing number of organizations are expanding their horizons with respect to restructuring by going beyond self-managing teams to higher levels of involvement (Lawler, 1992).

The data showing an increasing number of companies (from 65 to 74 percent) with employee committees that focus on policy and strategy issues are also consistent with the idea that companies are moving toward higher levels of involvement. Implemented effectively, this approach can give employees input on organization-wide policy and effectiveness issues.

Additional analysis of the data suggests that companies with job enrichment, self-managing work teams, and minibusiness units are more likely to have parallel-structure activities such as quality circles. In other words, companies that engage in one of the more popular employee involvement activities are also more likely to try the others.

However, as Table 6.3 shows, the use of multiple approaches on a large scale is not widespread. Only 43 percent of companies have tried two or more of seven possible approaches with over 40 percent of their employees. Even though this represents a significant increase from 1987 (when it was 19 percent), it is still a low figure. The most significant change is a large decrease in the percentage of companies who do not cover 40 percent or more of their employees with *any* power-sharing practices (from 58 percent in 1987 to 21 percent in 1996). Finally, it is important to note that as of 1996, a high percentage of these companies are using one or more power-sharing practices on a wide scale.

Figure 6.1 shows that decision-making power increasingly has been moved to lower levels as a result of involvement activities in these companies. This matches the survey results showing the growing popularity of the suggestion-oriented work design approaches to EI.

Overall, the data on the use of practices designed to move power downward in organizations show an interesting pattern. Suggestion-type

Table 6.3	Percentage of Companies Using Power-Sharing Approaches with More Than 40 Percent of Employees.			
Number of Approaches	1987 (*n* = 323)	1990 (*n* = 313)	1993 (*n* = 279)	1996 (*n* = 212)
0	58	52	33	21
1	23	28	30	36
2	11	13	17	19
3	6	4	12	11
4	3	3	5	9
5 or more	0	1	3	3

Seven possible kinds: survey feedback, job enrichment, quality circles, employee participation groups, union-management QWL committees, minibusiness units, self-managing work teams.

programs continue to be widely used. Most corporations have tried this approach somewhere within their organization. This is probably because these programs are the easiest to install and effect the least change in the power relationships in organizations.

We have no data that show why the use of quality circles is stable while the use of problem-solving groups is increasing. A reasonable guess is that corporations view quality circles as having significant problems with regard to the kind of issues they work on and to how the ideas they develop are implemented. Problem-solving groups often deal with these concerns by specifying what issues will be worked on and providing a sponsor and budget in order to aid acceptance of the suggested changes.

The growth of self-managing teams, minibusiness units, and policy groups is a highly significant change and indicates that a number of companies are going beyond problem-solving approaches. All three of these approaches call for involving employees in important business decisions.

Finally, it is important to note that none of the power-sharing practices in Tables 6.1 and 6.2 are employed throughout most companies. Typically they cover less than 40 percent of the employees in the companies that utilize them. This finding strongly suggests that companies are still piloting these practices or using them selectively

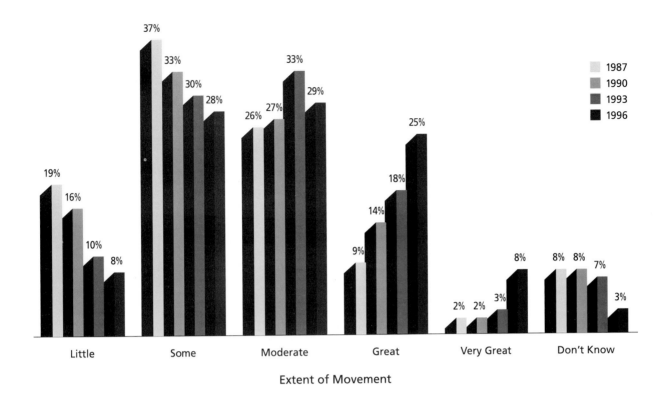

Figure 6.1 Percentage of Companies Indicating Extent to Which Decision Making Moved to Lower Levels as a Result of Employment Involvement.

rather than adopting them as their only approach to organizing and managing. For some practices, this decision is undoubtedly appropriate since they are not universally applicable. Nevertheless, it suggests that many companies are still not fully committed to creating high-involvement organizations. Change is occurring but at an incremental, not revolutionary, pace.

Employee Involvement, Total Quality Management, and Reengineering

Patterns of Employee Involvement

Employee involvement theory, reviewed in Section One, argues that to be effective, organizations must establish the right patterns of information sharing, knowledge building, rewards, and power distribution. In other words, it is not enough for organizations to implement power-sharing practices, or information sharing, or training programs, or new rewards systems. All of these are needed in appropriate amounts and patterns. Patterns of mutually reinforcing practices are necessary to encourage and sustain employee involvement in a business. Thus, the overall pattern of management practices is much more important than the individual practices. Individual practices need to fit together to produce a coherent approach to involvement.

In our 1990 study of Fortune 1000 firms (Lawler, Mohrman, and Ledford, 1992), for the first time we examined the patterns of EI practice adoption that the data revealed. Using a statistical technique called cluster analysis, we found that organizations using one EI practice tended to use all other EI practices to the same degree; that is, low users tended to be relatively low in their use of all practices, average users tended to be average in the use of all practices, and high users tended to be high in the use of all practices. A fourth type, consisting of reward-oriented users, was different. These firms were high in the use of reward and quality practices, but average in the use of other practices.

Our 1993 study took a different approach, which we duplicated in 1996. It examined three approaches to employee involvement by asking specifically how much these approaches were used.

Suggestion involvement entails the power to make suggestions for change but not necessarily the power to make decisions. Suggestion involvement usually is provided by means of parallel structures, such as improvement teams or participation groups, that supplement rather than replace existing structures. The teams depend on the existing management structure for the implementation of the changes they suggest. While team members often receive training, information, and recognition or rewards, such practices are typically not extended to employees who are not group members. As a result, this form of EI can be installed with relatively minor changes to the existing organization. In this sense, it represents a limited type of involvement.

Job involvement is based on changes in work design, offering employees more control over the day-to-day decisions that are relevant to their jobs. These changes are accomplished through the enrichment of individual jobs or the creation of self-managing work teams that do interdependent work. One key organizational design element—namely, work design—is automatically changed by this approach. Information sharing, training, and rewards may also be changed to support the new work design.

Business involvement encompasses job involvement and suggestion involvement but goes further; it stresses the involvement of employees in managing the business. Organizations practicing business involvement use a wide variety of mutually reinforcing power-sharing, information-sharing, skill-building, reward, and other human resources practices to support and facilitate the approach. The best-known examples are the showcase manufacturing plants built by such companies as Procter & Gamble, General Mills, Anheuser-Busch, and many others. The term *high performance organization* is often applied to this type. It is also called a high-involvement design.

We investigated the use of these three forms of employee involvement by asking respondents to answer the following question: "Approximately what percent of your corporation's employees are in units in which each of the following patterns of employee involvement practice is predominant?" They were asked to allocate 100 percent of the workforce to one or more of the five types, which are described in Table 7.1. The reader may note that we used the label "Improvement Teams" instead of "Suggestion Involvement," because previous feedback from some managers suggested that the latter might elicit a negative reaction. We added the category, "Other Form of Involvement," to capture kinds of employee involvement and combinations of employee involvement practices that did not fit our classification system.

The average number of employees in these firms who had no significant EI activities was 37 percent in 1993 and 36 percent in 1996. Improvement teams were the most popular form of employee involvement in both the 1993 and 1996 surveys. Next in popularity came job involvement and business involvement. The data show only a slight tendency for involvement patterns to change from 1993 to 1996. There appears to be slightly more use of job and business involvement and slightly less use of improvement teams. This is consistent with our results in Section Six that showed

Table 7.1	Percentage of Employees Covered by Different Employee Involvement Types.		
		1993	1996
None	No significant employee involvement exists in these parts of the corporation.	37	36
Improvement Teams	Employee involvement focuses on special groups that are responsible for recommending improvements to management. These groups may be participation groups, quality circles, quality action teams, union-management QWL committees, and so on. Members of the groups receive special training to enable them to work better as a team. They receive information relevant to the problems they are working on. There may be financial rewards or recognition for team suggestions.	31	26
Job Involvement	Employee involvement focuses on creating work designs that are highly motivating, such as self-managing teams. Training focuses on job-specific skills and/or team functioning. Employees receive information relevant to their performance as individuals and/or teams. The reward system may reinforce the job design emphasis; practices might include team performance incentives or pay increases for mastering skills that are needed within a team.	12	17
Business Involvement	Employees are involved heavily in the management of the business. Improvement teams and job involvement approaches may be used as part of this strategy. Self-managing work teams and perhaps minibusiness units are used extensively, and management routinely seeks employee input on policies and practices of the organization. Reward innovations are used, perhaps including gainsharing or profit sharing in the unit. Employees receive extensive training in job skills, team skills, and in business issues. Employees receive extensive business information, and they are expected to use it.	10	12
Other Form of Involvement	Employee involvement approaches not described above.	9	10

the changing patterns in the usage of different power-sharing approaches.

Overall, the results show that the typical employee is likely to experience some form of employee involvement, but it is likely to be a relatively low level of involvement. The most powerful and intense forms of involvement (job involvement and business involvement) still appear to cover only a relatively small percentage of the total U.S. workforce. Perhaps even more striking is the fact that over a third of the workforce still experiences no form of employee involvement at all.

There was tremendous variation in the use of involvement types from one firm to another. For this reason, we looked for a way to classify firms according to the pattern of involvement that they emphasized. Inspection of the data suggested a relatively simple classification procedure that covered all but twenty-nine companies in our sample (see Table 7.2). We classified any company that did not cover at least half of the workforce in any form of EI as "Low Employee Involvement." A firm that had at least a third of its employees in improvement teams was classified as emphasizing "Suggestion Involvement." A firm covering at least a third of its employees in the job involvement, business involvement, or other involvement forms was classified as using that form.

Although the threshold of one-third of the workforce for classification in one of the four types may seem low, the average firm in each category actually included a majority of its employees in that type. Firms in the "Business Involvement" type, for example, have an average of 54 percent of employees in units using this type of employee involvement. Comparable numbers for the other types of involvement are 50 percent for "Job Involvement," 63 percent for "Suggestion Involvement," 65 percent for "Other" involvement, and 79 percent for "No Involvement."

Table 7.2   Classification of Firms by Employee Involvement Type.

Employee Involvement Type	Firm Classified as This Type If Percent of Employees Is Greater Than or Equal to:	1993		1996	
		Number of Companies	Percent of Sample	Number of Companies	Percent of Sample
Low Employee Involvement	50% in no significant involvement effort	98	35	76	36
Suggestion Involvement	33% in improvement teams	93	33	47	22
Job Involvement	33% in job involvement	15	5	26	12
Business Involvement	33% in business involvement	16	6	17	8
Other Type of Involvement	33% in other type of involvement	21	8	17	8
Not Classified	NA	36	13	29	14

We can measure differences in the use of EI practices among the five types by considering their scores on five indices of EI practices. We developed indices, or summary scores, for information-sharing, knowledge-building, reward, and power-sharing practices. These four indices represent a composite measure of the degree to which companies are using various practices in each category. We also developed an overall EI index that is a combination of the other four indices. Resource C provides details on how these scores were calculated.

As can be seen in Table 7.3, the Low Involvement firms consistently make relatively low use of information, training, reward, and power-sharing practices. This does not mean that firms in this category use no employee involvement practices. They tend to employ all of them to some degree but make significantly less use of them than the other types do. The Suggestion Involvement, Job Involvement, and Business Involvement firms are consistent with our expectations about the practices they use. The results for business involvement and job involvement are similar with respect to knowledge, power, and overall involvement. They do differ, however, with respect to rewards and information; as expected, firms in the Business Involvement category use these practices more than do firms in the Job Involvement category. No clear picture of the Other Involvement type emerges from our analysis. It is lower than the other three types of involvement on all indices with the exception of information. Further inspection of specific cases indicates that firms in this type use a variety of idiosyncratic patterns rather than one homogeneous pattern.

Table 7.3	Mean Use of Involvement Practices by Employee Involvement Type.				
Indices	Low Involvement (n = 76)	Suggestion Involvement (n = 47)	Job Involvement (n = 26)	Business Involvement (n = 17)	Other Involvement (n = 17)
Information	4.3	4.8	5.0	5.2	4.9
Knowledge	2.6	3.5	3.5	3.6	3.1
Rewards	2.6	3.0	3.2	3.7	3.1
Power	2.2	3.0	3.1	3.0	2.6
Employee Involvement	2.9	3.5	3.8	3.7	3.4

Note: Numbers are mean responses to percent of employees covered by practice, using the following response scale: 1 = None (0 percent), 2 = Almost none (1–20 percent), 3 = Some (21–40 percent), 4 = About half (41–60 percent), 5 = Most (61–80 percent), 6 = Almost all (81–99 percent), 7 = All (100 percent).

Table 7.2 indicates that the two largest categories are Low Involvement and Suggestion Involvement, with 36 percent and 22 percent of firms, respectively. This means that over a third of Fortune 1000 firms have made no major commitment to employee involvement, and almost a quarter emphasize the form of employee involvement that requires the least organizational change. Twelve percent of the firms in the sample fall into the Job Involvement type while 8 percent fall into the Business Involvement type. This is consistent with data from prior studies indicating that more complex, deeper forms of employee involvement remain much less common.

A comparison of the 1993 and the 1996 firm classification by employee involvement type shows little change in the percentages. There is a slight decrease in the use of suggestion involvement and an increase in job involvement. This is consistent with the other data in this study, which show a trend away from suggestion involvement to higher levels of employee involvement. Still, the overall result is consistent with the conclusion that the more complex, deeper forms of employee involvement are less common.

SECTION 8

Total Quality Management

Total quality management (TQM) is a set of organizational strategies, practices, and tools for organizational performance improvement. A variety of practices are included under the general rubric of TQM. At the operational level, it includes the application of systematic approaches to the measurement and improvement of work processes to ensure that they are adding value and meeting the needs of the customer. Work simplification is often part and parcel of TQM, as organizations focus on eliminating steps that do not add value and on combining tasks to reduce the number of interfaces.

Many companies are collaborating with their suppliers as part of their efforts to improve quality. They recognize that quality problems often result from the delivery of supplies and raw material that do not meet process specifications and that supplier interfaces often include steps that do not add value. Although the focus in TQM is primarily on *quality,* defined as meeting the needs of the customer, this management approach also has cost, service, and schedule implications. The practice of monitoring the cost of quality links the quality- and customer-focused aspects of TQM to the financial or cost aspects of the organization. In order to create customer focus, TQM incorporates systematic customer satisfaction monitoring and direct exposure of employees to customers to ensure an understanding of their needs.

TQM was first applied in manufacturing settings, where it typically includes training front-line employees to use statistical process control methods to monitor and improve work processes and to inspect their own work. It also often includes just-in-time deliveries from suppliers to reduce inventory costs. Some organizations have redesigned the workplace into work cells that apply TQM techniques and that in many cases have the characteristics of self-managing teams. Some of the more production-oriented administrative and service operations also have adopted these TQM techniques and practices.

TQM also includes strategic elements—namely, the involvement of management in quality councils that link TQM activities to the key strategic focuses of the organization, and cross-functional planning that explicitly acknowledges and plans for interdependencies among functions. Process reengineering is often linked to total quality management (for example, Hammer and Champy, 1993; Davenport, 1993). It may result in the introduction of substantially different work processes. But instead of taking the process-improvement approach that is common in TQM, reengineering focuses on reconceptualizing what and how work is done, often by incorporating the capabilities of information technology. In practice, reengineering often equates to process simplification and lateral integration with a primary focus on downsizing. Because, as was discussed in Section One, it has developed its own identity, it will be treated separately in the next section.

The use of the TQM approach was on an upward trajectory in U.S. companies from the early 1970s to the mid–1990s. In our 1993 survey, 76 percent of companies reported having a TQM program (see Table 8.1). This compares with 73 percent in our 1990 survey and with 74 percent reported in a 1993 survey of human resource and quality respondents (Moran, Hogeveen, Latham, and Ross-Eft, 1994). The 1996 data show a significant drop in the percentage of companies with TQM programs, down to 66 percent.

The 1996 data also show a drop in the percent of employees covered by TQM programs. In our 1993 survey, TQM programs on average covered 50 percent of employees, compared with 41 percent in our 1996 survey, the same percentage that was covered in 1990. Finally, 19 percent of companies (compared to 18 percent in 1990 and 25 percent in 1993) report that all employees are covered by TQM programs. Overall, the results suggest that TQM efforts

	1990	1993	1996
Table 8.1 Total Quality Management Coverage.			
Percent of Companies with a TQM Program	73	76	66
Average Percent of Employees Covered	41	50	41
Percent of Companies with 100 Percent of Employees Covered	18	25	19

have returned to their 1990 level of use and are less widely utilized than they were in 1993.

Tables 8.2 and 8.3 present usage patterns for a number of common TQM practices. These tables include data from only those companies indicating that they have TQM programs. The practices are presented in three groupings that resulted from a statistical analysis to determine common usage patterns. The six practices in Table 8.2 are the core practices that tend to be adopted by most companies as they become increasingly involved in TQM. The four production-oriented practices in Table 8.3 constitute a related set of practices that tend to be used where the work is routine and measurable. Most often this means that they are used in manufacturing settings and in white-collar throughput-oriented environments. The patterns of adoption for each of the last two practices in Table 8.3 (cost-of-quality monitoring and collaboration with suppliers) do not relate to each other or to the preceding two clusters of practices. Thus, they are treated as individual practices in all analyses.

The use of work simplification and direct exposure to customers was measured in 1990, 1993, and 1996; a comparison shows that both have increased. Two-thirds of the companies with TQM programs use these practices in areas employing more than 20 percent of the workforce. The two most heavily used core practices are quality improvement teams and customer satisfaction monitoring. Both of these practices showed a slight decrease in use from 1993 to 1996. Four-fifths of companies use customer satisfaction monitoring in areas employing more than 20 percent of the workforce, and 22 percent cover more than 80 percent of all employees with this practice. Three-fourths use quality improvement teams with more than 20 percent of the workforce, and 8 percent cover all employees.

Table 8.2		Percentage of Employees Covered by Core TQM Practices.							
		Mean	None (0 percent)	Almost None (1–20 percent)	Some (21–40 percent)	About Half (41–60 percent)	Most (61–80 percent)	Almost All (81–99 percent)	All (100 percent)
Quality Improvement Teams	1993	3.88	3	21	20	22	14	15	5
	1996	3.73	1	25	28	16	13	8	8
Quality Councils	1993	2.95	20	35	14	12	5	8	5
	1996	2.65	22	33	23	12	5	2	4
Cross-Functional Planning	1993	2.82	13	38	26	8	10	4	2
	1996	2.62	21	34	24	9	7	2	2
Work Simplification	1990	3.02	13	26	33	12	7	7	0
	1993	3.23	8	28	28	17	8	6	4
	1996	3.44	8	23	28	18	15	5	4
Customer Satisfaction Monitoring	1993	4.23	1	15	25	18	13	18	10
	1996	3.99	2	16	24	21	15	18	4
Direct Employee Exposure to Customers	1990	3.11	4	32	31	16	4	4	0
	1993	3.29	2	31	33	16	11	6	2
	1996	3.39	1	28	35	15	12	7	2

Note: Questions were not asked in 1987. Not all questions were asked in 1990. Mean is based on a seven-point scale.

The least frequently used core practices are quality councils and cross-functional planning. Fewer than half of the companies use them with more than 20 percent of the workforce. It is significant that these less frequently employed practices are those that are more strategic in nature and involve higher-level direction and involvement. Both of these items showed a decreased rate of use from 1993 to 1996.

The four production-oriented practices in Table 8.3 all experienced increases from 1990 to 1996. The most frequently used is self-inspection, a practice that covers more than 20 percent of employees in two-thirds of the companies. Statistical process control by front-line employees and just-in-time deliveries are used by over half of the companies in areas covering more than 20 percent of the employees.

Table 8.3 **Percentage of Employees Covered by Production and Other TQM Practices.**

		Mean	None (0 percent)	Almost None (1–20 percent)	Some (21–40 percent)	About Half (41–60 percent)	Most (61–80 percent)	Almost All (81–99 percent)	All (100 percent)
Production-Oriented Practices									
Self-Inspection	1990	3.19	10	25	31	14	7	7	0
	1993	3.38	7	27	27	14	15	8	3
	1996	3.63	8	24	21	13	20	8	6
Statistical Control Method Used by Front-Line Employees	1993	2.82	12	38	27	11	7	5	1
	1996	2.96	16	30	23	14	10	5	2
Just-in-Time Deliveries	1990	2.63	24	31	22	11	4	4	2
	1993	2.88	17	29	26	13	8	6	1
	1996	3.20	10	33	19	16	12	7	3
Work Cells or Manufacturing Cells	1990	2.14	41	27	19	9	2	2	0
	1993	2.23	35	33	14	14	3	2	0
	1996	2.50	30	29	21	10	5	5	1
Other Practices									
Cost-of-Quality Monitoring	1990	2.73	18	35	24	11	4	4	3
	1993	2.78	17	37	20	13	6	5	2
	1996	2.83	19	32	22	14	6	4	4
Collaboration with Suppliers in Quality Efforts	1990	2.80	13	37	27	11	3	3	2
	1993	3.39	5	28	27	16	13	8	3
	1996	3.47	4	31	22	16	13	10	3

Note: Questions not asked in 1987. Not all questions were asked in 1990. Mean is based on a 1–7 scale.

The least frequently used practice is work cells; they are not used at all by 30 percent of companies and are employed by only a little over one-third of companies in areas with more than 20 percent of their employees.

The relatively low usage pattern of the production-oriented practices no doubt reflects the fact that they are only applicable to the production-oriented areas of a company. These practices may in fact cover a large percentage of the appropriate employees, given that less than 35 percent of the employees in these companies are involved in manufacturing operations. It is also significant that their usage continues to increase. Apparently they are proving to be important parts of TQM programs in manufacturing settings.

The use of cost-of-quality monitoring shows little increase. Fewer than half the companies use it with more than 20 percent of their employees. In contrast, collaboration with suppliers in quality efforts experienced the largest and most significant overall gain of any practice from 1990 to 1996. Almost two-thirds of companies used it with more than 20 percent of their employees, up from one-half of the companies in the 1990 survey. The increased implementation of this practice is particularly interesting because it always involves two or more organizations. It provides evidence of how strongly TQM thinking is affecting the way manufacturing organizations are operating today.

Overall, the 1996 survey results suggest some interesting conclusions about what is happening to total quality management programs. First, fewer companies seem to have formal TQM programs. On the other hand, the results suggest that those that do are using more and more TQM practices. This seems to be particularly true of collaboration with suppliers, work cells, just-in-time deliveries, and self-inspection.

On average, about 40 percent of the employees in a firm with a TQM program are covered by it. The usage patterns for particular practices vary considerably, with only a few companies employing any of the practices for all its employees. Quality improvement teams and customer satisfaction monitoring remain the most extensively employed. In general, the operational aspects of TQM are the most widely used. The strategic approaches that require top management involvement, such as the creation of quality councils and cross-functional planning, are used less frequently.

It is impossible to determine from our 1996 results whether there is increased usage of the TQM practices among companies that do not have total quality management programs, since we did not ask these respondents to indicate their usage of specific TQM practices. A good guess, however, is that some or all of them are being used increasingly by companies that do not have formal TQM programs. For example, measuring customer satisfaction is becoming a more frequently used practice; it has developed a life of its own, independent of its tie to TQM.

One way of summarizing what seems to be happening with the total quality management approach is that it has found its niche and is becoming increasingly popular within that niche. Companies that adopt it are finding that it makes sense to adopt not one but a whole set of practices that support their total quality management effort. On the other hand, there is no evidence that more companies are adopting total quality management programs, and at this point, there is little reason to suspect that in the future more will. In this sense, TQM may have peaked and even be in slight decline. This is not to say, however, that the specific practices associated with TQM are going to be used less frequently. They are likely to be used not only by companies that remain committed to overall total quality management efforts but by companies who simply find them to be approaches that offer support for their way of managing. This trend may mean that TQM programs will disappear, killed off by their success in convincing companies that the practices they advocate should be standard operating procedures.

SECTION 9

Process Reengineering

Process reengineering has only recently become a popular approach to improving organizational performance. As our discussion in Section One highlighted, it is a newcomer compared to employee involvement and total quality management. Judging by the attention reengineering has received in magazines, journals, and books, it is likely that many corporations have utilized—and still are utilizing—it.

Our 1996 survey included a series of questions on reengineering. Our intention in including these items for the first time was simple: to gather data that might shed some light on this popular and frequently debated management approach. Table 9.1 shows the results of a question that asked companies to indicate what percent of their employees are in work units that have experienced process reengineering efforts. The results confirm the widely held view that process reengineering has indeed been used in many American corporations in the last few years, as 81 percent of the companies

Table 9.1	Process Reengineering Coverage in 1996.
Percent of Companies with Program	81
Average Percent of Employees Covered	38
Percent with 100 Percent of Employees Covered	10

report that at least some of their employees are affected by reengineering. In most cases, reengineering efforts affected less than half of the employees in the companies with reengineering efforts (38 percent on average), but in 10 percent of the companies, they affected 100 percent of the employees. In many ways, these are astoundingly high impact levels for a new organizational improvement method that was only a few years old in 1996. It is hardly surprising, given its rapid growth, that reengineering is often subject to so much attention and criticism.

We also asked those companies that reported having process reengineering efforts to identify the changes that were made as a part of these efforts. A statistical analysis clustered the items into two groups, as shown in Table 9.2.

Given the close tie between process reengineering and the adoption of information technology, we were not surprised that the most common change in process reengineering efforts is the redesign of a company's information systems. The next three most likely changes are generally consistent with the popular image of process reengineering efforts. They include doing the same work with fewer people, doing the same work with less supervision, and an overall lower cost structure. The latter, of course, follows directly from having less supervision and fewer people.

It may be a little surprising to see that reengineering efforts frequently result in having less supervision, since reengineering is not particularly associated with the idea of employee involvement and self-management. It is impossible to tell whether the reduction in supervision is a result of information technology making fewer supervisors necessary—restructuring the work so that less coordinating is necessary on the part of supervisors—or whether it is done to involve employees in decision making and improve the quality of work life of employees. A good guess, however, is that the reduction in supervision is more likely to be associated with a desire to reduce overhead costs than a desire to create more involvement and a better quality of work life for employees. This conclusion is generally

Table 9.2

Percentage of Companies Adopting Reengineering Practices.

	Mean	Little or No Extent	Some Extent	Moderate Extent	Great Extent	Very Great Extent
Work Structure						
Process Simplification	3.2	3	22	34	36	6
Creation of Cross-Functional Units	3.0	12	24	30	25	9
Major Information System Redesign	3.3	8	22	19	32	19
Enriched Multiskilled Individual Jobs	2.7	12	32	37	16	3
Multiskilled Teams	2.7	14	32	32	18	5
Cost Reduction						
Doing Same Work with Fewer People	3.4	4	16	30	34	17
Doing Same Work with Less Supervision	3.3	6	19	32	30	13
Lower Overall Cost Structure	3.2	5	23	31	27	14

Note: Mean is based on a five-point scale.

supported by the finding that enriched, multiskilled jobs and multiskilled teams are the least common changes in process reengineering efforts. These can be powerful sources of motivation and employee involvement.

Finally, process reengineering efforts are moderately likely to create cross-functional units. It is somewhat surprising that this result is not stronger, given the heavy emphasis on multifunctional units in the literature on process reengineering. Like process simplification, it is frequently called a key component of reengineering.

Since comparable data on reengineering were not collected in earlier surveys, we cannot make any definitive statements about the growth of process reengineering. In our 1993 study, we did ask whether organizations had engaged in process reengineering as part of their total quality management programs. A significant number of companies responded that they had. Ninety-two percent of the companies that had TQM programs had engaged in some process reengineering. At that point, 76 percent of all corporations had a TQM program. Thus, we can deduce that around 70 percent of the companies in 1993 had a reengineering effort. But at that time it was more common for companies to adopt other total quality management practices than adopt process reengineering. For example, quality improvement teams and customer satisfaction monitoring were used by a higher percentage of the companies than was reengineering. In any case, the data from 1993 suggest that some process reengineering was already going on, though certainly not to the extent suggested by our 1996 data.

It is hard to imagine that much process reengineering activity would have been reported in 1990 if we had asked about it. Process reengineering is clearly a "1990s happening" in American business—a happening that has affected most corporations and many of the people within those corporations.

<hr />

SECTION 10

Relationships Among Employee Involvement, Total Quality Management, and Reengineering

We took an initial look at the similarities and differences among employee involvement, total quality management, and reengineering in Section One. There we pointed out that the employee involvement and TQM literatures share an emphasis on the use of participation groups that utilize problem-solving and decision-making tools (see also Lawler, 1994; Lawler, 1996; Mohrman, Galbraith, and Lawler, 1998). They both emphasize performance feedback and information sharing, although TQM tends to focus primarily on process feedback and customer information while the employee involvement literature focuses more on business results and other business information. TQM provides management tools that emphasize the control and improvement of work processes and gears activities to customer requirements. Employee involvement emphasizes the motivational system in the organization, including the design of motivating jobs and ways of setting goals and reviewing and rewarding of performance. It also focuses on the design of teams and business units to enable employee involvement in the business.

TQM and employee involvement can complement one another. TQM requires that the organization be designed and managed for involvement so that people can improve its performance, and it provides the tools to facilitate these goals.

Reengineering shares some characteristics with both EI and TQM. For example, it focuses on the importance of lateral relationships and on decreasing the number of management levels. But it typically places less emphasis on employee participation and teams than does either EI or TQM.

It is one thing to point out the similarities and differences among EI, TQM, and reengineering; it is quite another to combine them effectively within an organization. Managers must deal with a number of key issues, such as where to start, how to explain the relationships among the various activities, and what pattern of practices to put it into place. This section will focus on these issues by reviewing data from a series of questions concerning the relationship among EI, TQM, and process reengineering.

Employee Involvement and Total Quality Management. Figure 10.1 presents the results from three questions on how companies manage the relationship between TQM and EI programs. In 1996, 38 percent of companies said that their TQM programs started first, while about 36 percent said EI started first. This pattern was the reverse of 1990s, when EI programs were more likely to have started first. Thus, the data suggest growth in the use of TQM as a lead change program.

In 1996, 47 percent of companies managed EI and TQM as one integrated program, while 21 percent simply coordinated them. This marks a significant increase in the percentage of companies managing the two approaches as an integrated program, as it is up from 36 percent in 1990. Apparently companies are more and more recognizing the complementary nature of these two programs.

TQM is the primary focus in most programs. Eighty percent of companies in 1993 and 69 percent in 1996 saw involvement as part of TQM. However, an increasing number report quality is a part of employee involvement. This finding suggests that although most companies are adopting EI practices to assist TQM activities, there may be a growing tendency to use TQM practices as part of EI programs.

There is a strong correlation between the adoption of employee involvement approaches and the use of TQM practices (see Table 10.1). The extent to which companies employ the core TQM practices, the production-oriented practices, collaboration with customers, and cost-of-quality monitoring all have a highly significant relationship to the overall employee involvement index in both 1993 and 1996. The relationship to the development of knowledge and skills is particularly strong, demonstrating the heavy emphasis

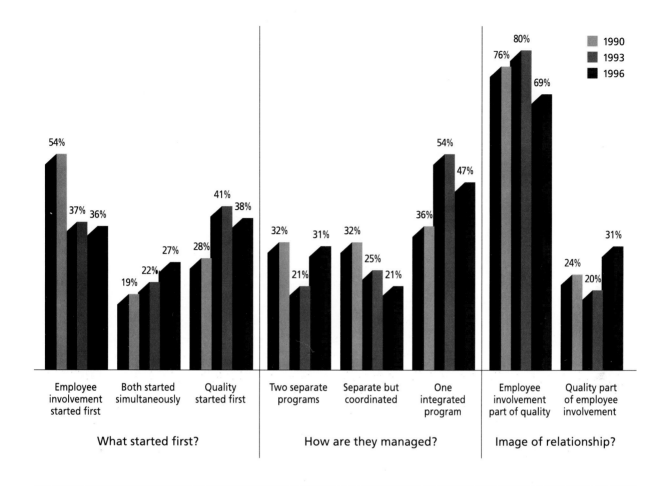

Figure 10.1   Relationship of Employee Involvement to Total Quality Management.

in TQM programs on the development of skills. TQM's relationship to power sharing is also very strong, reflecting the focus on problem-solving and decision-making groups in TQM in general and on work cells and teams.

The relationship between TQM and information sharing is substantially weaker than the one for knowledge and skill development. Apparently many TQM programs are stressing training in the use of improvement tools and power sharing at the operator level but are not going beyond that to share important business information with employees.

There is no overall strong relationship in either 1993 or 1996 between the use of TQM practices and the use of involvement-oriented reward practices. Only two of the individual TQM practices, self-inspection and work simplification, are significantly related to the reward index. Companies that are practicing self-inspection and

	Table 10.1		Relationship Between EI Indices and TQM Practices (Correlation Coefficients).							

	EI Overall		Information Sharing		Knowledge and Skills Development		Rewards		Power Sharing	
TQM Practices	1993	1996	1993	1996	1993	1996	1993	1996	1993	1996
Core Practices Overall	.41***	.49***	.29***	.23*	.50***	.47***	.13	.23*	.48***	.54***
Quality Improvement Teams	.24***	.30***	.08	.13	.32***	.36***	.11	.13	.32***	.45***
Quality Councils	.20**	.22*	.12	.18*	.30***	.30***	.06	.01	.27***	.20*
Cross-Functional Planning	.38***	.38***	.24***	.25**	.47***	.42***	.13	.18*	.47***	.39***
Work Simplification	.38***	.44***	.23***	.12	.44***	.42***	.18	.30***	.38***	.48***
Customer Satisfaction Monitoring	.35***	.35***	.32***	.20*	.38***	.28***	.06	.12	.41***	.36***
Direct Employee Exposure to Customers	.30***	.34***	.31***	.26**	.36***	.28***	.08	.15	.34***	.32***
Production-Oriented Practices Overall	.39***	.48***	.22***	.29**	.51***	.54***	.16	.18	.40***	.53***
Self-Inspection	.36***	.49***	.21**	.22*	.42***	.48***	.20**	.26**	.34***	.47***
Statistical Control Method Used by Front-Line Employees	.36***	.30***	.16	.21*	.47***	.50***	.11	.04	.36***	.38***
Just-in-Time Deliveries	.25**	.35***	.19**	.24**	.38***	.35***	.13	.14	.23**	.34***
Work Cells or Manufacturing Cells	.28***	.36***	.13	.31***	.37***	.36***	.08	.03	.34***	.40***
Other Practices										
Cost-of-Quality Monitoring	.34**	.24**	.22**	.18*	.36***	.31***	.17	.05	.32***	.35***
Collaboration with Suppliers in Quality Efforts	.39***	.40***	.26***	.24**	.47***	.32***	.11	.15	.41***	.39***
Percentage of Employees Covered	.28***	.31***	.12	.14*	.35***	.35***	.05	.12	.35***	.34***

Note: See Resource C for explanation of indices.
Key: * = weak relationship (p ≤ .05)
 ** = moderate relationship (p ≤ .01)
 *** = strong relationship (p ≤ .001)

work simplification are more likely to link rewards to performance. This may be because with these practices, they recognize it is important to use pay as an incentive. The lack of a relationship with rewards suggests that companies that employ TQM are not making employees stakeholders in business performance. TQM for most employees does not appear to mean a business partnership.

Work simplification is strongly related to power sharing and to knowledge and skills development. This suggests that work simplification is not leading inexorably to simple, unenriched jobs; quite the opposite appears to be true. Self-inspection, often a part of work simplification, is also associated with knowledge and skills development and with power sharing.

An interesting finding is the strong relationship of cross-functional planning to the EI indices. The creation of planning processes that extend across the organization appears to result in more opportunities for people to be informed about their company, develop knowledge and skills, and participate in empowered decision-making forums.

Table 10.2 shows the patterns of adoption of TQM practices by companies in each of the different employee involvement types discussed in Section Seven. The most common type of employee participation is suggestion involvement. Companies that use suggestion involvement are especially high in the use of improvement teams, as well as customer satisfaction monitoring and self-inspection. Suggestion involvement relies primarily on the use of quality teams, so this result is not a surprise; teams are a way of getting employees to participate, yet they involve less of a commitment to many of the other aspects of TQM.

Companies that stress job involvement in their EI programs make the greatest use of customer satisfaction monitoring and self-inspection, both of which have job design ramifications. Companies with the most complex and complete form of employee involvement—business involvement—make the greatest use of most of the core and production-oriented approaches to TQM. They make the greatest use of direct exposure to customers, self-inspection, just-in-time deliveries, and collaboration with suppliers in TQM efforts. Business involvement entails employee participation in both the internal and external aspects of the organization, as the higher-scoring TQM practices for this type reflect.

In both 1993 and 1996, companies that report having no employee involvement initiative that covers the majority of their employees

Table 10.2 — Use of TQM Practices by Different Employee Involvement Types.

TQM Practices[1]	None 1993	None 1996	Suggestion Involvement 1993	Suggestion Involvement 1996	Job Involvement 1993	Job Involvement 1996	Business Involvement 1993	Business Involvement 1996	Other (unspecified) 1993	Other (unspecified) 1996
Core Practices Overall	2.7	2.6	3.6	4.1	3.9	3.4	4.5	3.8	3.1	3.2
Quality Improvement Teams	2.8	2.9	4.5	4.8	3.9	3.7	4.7	4.3	3.8	3.2
Quality Councils	2.3	2.1	3.4	3.6	2.8	2.5	4.4	2.8	2.0	2.3
Cross-Functional Planning	2.1	1.8	3.0	3.2	3.5	3.0	4.1	3.5	2.8	2.7
Work Simplification	2.5	2.3	3.4	4.3	4.6	3.6	4.7	4.0	3.2	3.6
Customer Satisfaction Monitoring	3.7	3.3	4.5	4.7	4.7	4.4	5.5	3.6	4.1	3.8
Direct Employee Exposure to Customers	3.1	3.0	3.3	3.8	3.4	3.1	4.5	4.3	3.1	3.6
Production-Oriented Practices Overall	2.3	2.2	3.0	3.5	3.3	3.4	3.5	3.9	2.6	3.3
Self-Inspection	2.6	2.4	3.7	4.5	4.2	4.2	4.6	4.5	3.4	3.4
Statistical Control Method Used by Front-Line Employees	2.3	2.2	3.2	3.5	2.9	3.4	3.1	3.4	2.6	2.6
Just-in-Time Deliveries	2.6	2.3	3.1	3.7	3.0	3.1	3.9	3.9	2.5	3.9
Work Cells or Manufacturing Cells	1.8	1.8	2.3	2.7	3.0	2.7	2.5	3.6	1.9	3.3
Other Practices										
Cost-of-Quality Monitoring	2.2	2.2	3.0	3.3	3.9	3.1	3.5	3.3	2.4	2.7
Collaboration with Suppliers in Quality Efforts	2.7	2.6	3.8	4.1	3.7	4.0	4.2	3.8	3.1	3.6
Percentage of Employees Covered	26	24	71	68	60	52	57	51	55	28

[1]Mean score on a scale from 1–7.

are those that also report the least TQM activity. Companies in the "Other" category seem to employ just-in-time deliveries and work cells at a relatively high level compared to the other involvement approaches. Overall, however, there appears to be little overlap with TQM, as companies falling into the "Other" category cover a relatively low percentage of their employees with TQM practices.

In sum, most companies have both employee involvement and TQM initiatives. They are most frequently coordinated or managed as one integrated program. Companies that have EI practices applied to large parts of their population tend also to use TQM practices extensively. Companies with business involvement have the broadest application of other performance improvement approaches.

Employee Involvement and Reengineering. Table 10.3 shows the relationship between the EI indices and the adoption of specific reengineering practices. There are a number of significant relationships. EI overall is particularly strongly related to the adoption of work structure changes. It is less strongly but still significantly related to the adoption of several cost reduction practices. Information sharing, knowledge development, and power sharing tend to be related to the use of reengineering practices, but rewards are not.

The results for the work restructuring practices are not surprising. In order to operate successfully, these approaches require employees to be more involved in their work and to take more responsibility for how it is done. The results for power sharing, which show strong correlations with work restructuring, as do knowledge and skills development, support this conclusion. These results clearly confirm that activities like creating multiskilled teams and redesigning information systems are associated with the use of greater sharing of power and the development of knowledge and skills. The adoption of reward system practices is not significantly related to work structure changes. This is a bit surprising since some of the reward system practices (such as skill-based pay) fit with the work system changes.

The results for cost reduction follow the same general pattern as do those for work structure. Cost reduction is strongly associated with knowledge and skills development and with the adoption of power-sharing practices. However, it is not associated with the adoption of reward system practices oriented toward employee involvement or with the adoption of information-sharing practices. The underlying explanation would appear to be that when cost reduction is the major target, organizations feel that they have to train the remaining workers to be more flexible and capable and that they inevitably have to share more power with them because there is less supervision available to "control them."

It is somewhat surprising that organizations do not change the reward system in order to reinforce people for operating successfully in a lower cost environment, nor do they share information with them about the results of cost reduction efforts. This raises the obvious issue of why everyone in reengineering efforts doesn't participate in whatever cost reduction savings are realized. It also suggests at least one reason why reengineering efforts are seen as having a negative effect on employees: the workers experience the reductions but do not participate in the gains.

Table 10.3   **Relationship Between EI Indices and Reengineering Practices (Correlation Coefficients).**

Reengineering Practices	EI Overall	Information Sharing	Knowledge and Skills Development	Rewards	Power Sharing
Work Structure	.40***	.27***	.39***	.08	.37***
Process Simplification Functional Units	.31***	.23**	.28***	.01	.25***
Creation of Cross-Functional Units	.35***	.23**	.33***	.08	.33***
Major Information System Redesign	.27***	.17*	.22**	.10	.26***
Enriched Multiskilled Individual Jobs	.30***	.19*	.31	.08	.27***
Multiskilled Teams	.29***	.22**	.36***	.01	.31***
Cost Reduction	.24**	.02	.32***	.01	.31***
Doing Same Work with Fewer People	.22**	.01	.29***	.00	.28***
Doing Same Work with Less Supervision	.19	–.00	.30***	–.06	.30***
Lower Overall Cost Structure	.24**	.04	.28***	.08	.25***
Percent Covered	.24***	.10	.24***	.07	.31***

Key: * = weak relationship (p ≤ .05)
     ** = moderate relationship (p ≤ .01)
     *** = strong relationship (p ≤ .001)

Reengineering and Total Quality Management. Table 10.4 shows the relationship between the adoption of TQM practices and reengineering practices. The relationships are consistently positive, and many are significant. They tend to be strongest for the work structure items, indicating a high degree of overlap between what are called reengineering practices and those considered TQM practices. In the work structure area, the weakest relationships are with major information system redesign, which is not a major theme in TQM. Thus it is not surprising that it is relatively unrelated to the adoption of a number of TQM practices. On the other hand, the adoption of process simplification and cross-functional units is strongly related to all of the TQM practices that we studied.

| Table 10.4 | Relationship of Reengineering to TQM Practices (Correlation Coefficients). | | | | |

Reengineering Practices	Core Practices Overall	Production-Oriented Practices	Cost-of-Quality Monitoring	Collaboration with Suppliers in Quality Efforts	Percent TQM Covered
Work Structure	.45***	.50***	.41***	.33***	.06
Process Simplification	.45***	.32***	.37***	.43***	.07
Creation of Cross-Functional Units	.41***	.50***	.43***	.33***	.10
Major Information System Redesign	.33***	.21*	.23*	.18*	.07
Enriched Multiskilled Individual Jobs	.31***	.44***	.29**	.22*	−.04
Multiskilled Teams	.24	.44***	.29**	.12	.04
Cost Reduction	.36***	.37***	.23*	.29**	.06
Doing Same Work with Fewer People	.29**	.31**	.19*	.29**	.06
Doing Same Work with Less Supervision	.29**	.31**	.20*	.21*	.00
Lower Overall Cost Structure	.38***	.38***	.24**	.30***	.09
Percent Covered	.31***	.17	.03	.10	.18**

Key: * = weak relationship (p ≤ .05)
    ** = moderate relationship (p ≤ .01)
    *** = strong relationship (p ≤ .001)

The cost reduction reengineering items show consistently significant relationships to the TQM practices. Apparently, the core TQM practices, the production-oriented practices, cost-of-quality monitoring, and collaboration with suppliers all tend to be included among the activities that are combined with most reengineering practices. In many respects, this is not surprising; quality consultants often emphasize that improving quality leads to an overall lowering of the cost structure of the business. It can also lead to organizations doing the same work with fewer people because of a reduced need for rework. And it can lead to less supervision if individuals become better at monitoring their own work and at managing themselves.

Integration of Reengineering. Reengineering programs may or may not be integrated with total quality management and employee involvement programs. There is nothing about the origin of reengineering programs that would suggest they should necessarily be integrated with either or both. Figure 10.2 shows that in 1996 the most common situation was to implement reengineering as a stand-alone program. The second most common (39 percent) was to integrate it with both TQM and EI. In a relatively small number of cases, reengineering was integrated with just TQM or with just EI.

The key question here is whether it makes any difference whether reengineering programs are integrated with EI or TQM programs. Table 10.5 provides some data that begin to answer this question. It compares the extent to which reengineering practices are adopted in

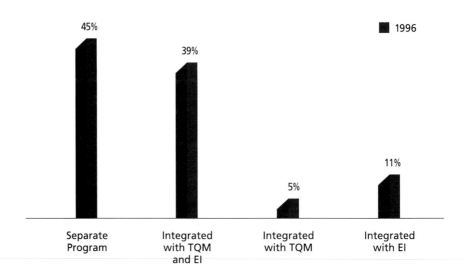

Figure 10.2   Integration of Reengineering Program with EI and TQM.

Table 10.5 **Adoption of Reengineering Practices with Different Approaches to Integrating Reengineering.**[1]

Reengineering Practices	Integration of Reengineering			
	A Separate Program	Integrated with Both TQM and EI	Integrated with TQM Only	Integrated with EI Only
Work Structure	2.7	3.2	2.7	3.2
Process Simplification	2.9	3.5	2.9	3.2
Creation of Cross-Functional Units	2.6	3.2	2.3	3.6
Major Information System Redesign	3.3	3.3	3.3	3.4
Enriched Multiskilled Individual Jobs	2.5	2.9	2.4	2.8
Multiskilled Teams	2.4	3.1	2.4	2.9
Cost Reduction	3.1	3.6	3.3	3.1
Doing Same Work with Fewer People	3.3	3.8	3.2	3.1
Doing Same Work with Less Supervision	2.9	3.6	3.4	3.3
Lower Overall Cost Structure	3.0	3.5	3.3	3.1
Percentage of Employees Covered	39	55	52	48

[1]Mean score on a scale of 1–5.

situations where different kinds of integration have occurred among reengineering, TQM, and EI. The results do not show large differences, but there are some interesting patterns.

In the work structuring area, integration with EI seems to be a critical factor in the extent of reengineering adoption. This is true whether the integration is with EI alone or with both EI and TQM. The association with EI tends to lead to more use of process simplification, cross-functional units, multiskilled teams, and enriched multiskilled jobs. This result is particularly interesting since it suggests that when there is little focus on EI, reengineering is more likely to create traditional simplified, standardized jobs rather than the type of motivating and enriched work associated with employee involvement.

The results associated with cost reduction show that integrating TQM and employee involvement has a significant impact on the type of cost reduction activities that occur. Specifically, there is a tendency to have less supervision, fewer employees, and a lower overall cost structure when these programs are integrated. This may well be an indication that the most powerful approach to cost reduction is an integrated TQM and employee involvement focus. Thus, TQM, EI, and reengineering put together may well be the best way to design organizations so that they are both more efficient and they involve employees taking greater responsibility.

Table 10.6 shows how the adoption of EI is related to the type of relationship that exists among reengineering, TQM, and EI. The results show a generally higher use of employee involvement practices when reengineering is integrated with both TQM and EI. One exception to the general rule involves rewards. Reward-oriented EI practices tend to be adopted to essentially the same degree regardless of how reengineering programs are integrated with TQM and EI.

The results for the relationship between the integration of reengineering programs and the adoption of total quality management

Table 10.6	Adoption of Employee Involvement Practices with Different Approaches to Integrating Reengineering.[1]			
	Integration of Reengineering			
	A Separate Program	Integrated with Both TQM and EI	Integrated with TQM Only	Integrated with EI Only
EI Overall	3.2	3.7	3.6	3.4
Information Sharing	4.6	4.9	5.0	4.8
Knowledge and Skills Development	2.9	3.5	3.3	2.9
Rewards	3.0	3.1	3.0	3.1
Power Sharing	2.4	3.2	2.9	2.7

[1]Mean score on a scale of 1–7.

TQM Practices	A Separate Program	Integrated with Both TQM and EI	Integrated with TQM Only	Integrated with EI Only
		Integration of Reengineering		
Core Practices Overall	3.0	3.7	3.1	2.9
Quality Improvement Teams	3.4	4.4	3.4	3.2
Quality Councils	2.7	2.9	2.1	2.0
Cross-Functional Planning	2.2	3.0	2.9	2.8
Work Simplification	3.0	4.1	2.7	3.2
Customer Satisfaction Monitoring	3.8	4.2	4.0	3.0
Direct Employee Exposure to Customers	3.1	3.6	4.0	3.4
Production-Oriented Practices Overall	2.8	3.4	2.4	2.9
Self-Inspection	3.1	4.3	3.3	3.2
Statistical Control Method Used by Front-Line Employees	2.8	3.2	1.9	2.8
Just-in-Time Deliveries	3.0	3.3	3.0	3.4
Work Cells or Manufacturing Cells	2.4	2.8	1.6	2.0
Other Practices				
Cost-of-Quality Monitoring	2.7	3.0	2.4	2.4
Collaboration with Suppliers in Quality Efforts	3.2	3.8	2.9	3.8
Percentage of Employees Covered	39	61	57	6

[1]Mean score on a scale of 1–7.

practices are presented in Table 10.7. These results are similar to those for employee involvement. TQM practices are most commonly implemented where reengineering is integrated with both TQM and EI. It is perhaps somewhat surprising that having reengineering integrated with TQM does not lead to as high a use rate as when TQM and EI are both integrated with reengineering. This finding further reinforces the argument for a potential synergy among reengineering, total quality management, and employee involvement. Combined with the finding that integration also leads to the highest adoption of both reengineering practices and employee involvement practices, these data strongly reinforce the view that integrated change efforts lead to the greatest amount of organizational change. These results also make it quite clear that EI, TQM, and reengineering can be implemented together.

PART THREE

Organizational Change: Practices and Strategy

One element that is common to employee involvement, total quality management, and reengineering is a change in the traditional employment relationship between individuals and organizations. We are not speaking here of a legal document to which an individual and an organization agree but of the psychological commitment that an organization makes to an individual and that an individual makes to an organization (Rousseau, 1995). William H. Whyte's book, *The Organization Man,* which was published in 1955, does a good job of outlining the traditional contract between large organizations and individuals. Whyte focuses on IBM, but similar contracts existed in AT&T, Exxon, and a host of other large U.S. companies. This "loyalty contract," as it has often been described, promised individuals a lifetime, paternalistic relationship with their organization in return for their commitment to that organization and for doing what they were told. In most companies this contract applied primarily to management and technical employees. Production and nonmanagement employees typically enjoyed less job security and fewer opportunities for development.

Many of the features of employee involvement, TQM, and particularly reengineering run counter to the traditional employment contract. Not only do they require individuals to learn new skills and competencies but they fundamentally change the conditions of the employment relationship in a number of other areas. Overall, individuals are expected to be more responsible for themselves and their careers and to add value in ways that justify their continued employment. Much of the paternalism of the traditional employment contract is gone, and individuals are valued more for skills, competencies, and performance than for loyalty. In addition, much of the job security that characterized the traditional relationship is gone. The key question is no longer what have you done for me but what can you do for me in the future.

One of the first questions that arises in the current business environment is whether organizations have moved toward a formal statement of the new employment relationship as part of their change process. Responses to our survey question on this issue showed that only 33 percent of the companies in the Fortune 1000 actually have a formal statement of their social or employment contract. Of course, concerns about making a commitment that could lead to legal liability may be responsible for this situation. It also may be that organizations are unclear as to what kind of statement can be made in these turbulent times. When asked in our survey whether there is a clear contract, a significant number said that their company is changing so fast it is not clear what the contract is. Finally, organizations may feel that the statement that they would have to make in this era of downsizing is so unattractive that it is better left unsaid.

Interestingly enough, when asked about their formal written contract, the majority (57 percent) of the companies that have one said that it was new in the last three years. Although this represents only a small portion of the all the firms, it is an interesting finding. This is a good indication that the old employment contract is no longer applicable and that some companies are actively trying to establish a new one.

Table 11.1 shows how companies describe the new employment contract. The first four questions address the issue of employment stability and security. Not surprisingly, given the data reported earlier about the amount of change occurring, in corporations no one has a secure job or a job for life. Instead, corporations increasingly see themselves as meritocracies in which performance and skills are the keys to maintaining employment—providing, of course, that business conditions justify employing someone.

The meritocracy theme comes through strongly in the four items concerning what is rewarded. Seniority is clearly not rewarded significantly, nor is loyalty. Instead, rewards are tied to individual and group and/or organizational performance.

The two questions on responsibility for career development and performance show a lack of support for a paternalistic model. The clear response is that employees are expected to develop themselves and their careers and to a moderate extent manage their own performance. Career management is no longer the responsibility of the organization or management.

The final three questions address the issue of the appropriateness of the employment contracts that firms have. Generally, the attitudes are favorable toward them. Respondents see them as fitting the business strategy fairly well. These contracts are also, though to a lesser degree, seen as being understood by most employees. Finally, respondents report that employees typically are moderately satisfied with their employment contracts. This may be an overstatement

Table 11.1

Percentage of Companies Operating by Different Employment Contract Practices.

Employment Contract Corporations Operate by	Mean[1]	Little or No Extent	Some Extent	Moderate Extent	Great Extent	Very Great Extent
Continued Employment of Individuals Based on Performance	4.0	1	4	20	48	28
Continued Employment of Individuals Based on Continual Development of Skills and Knowledge	3.4	3	15	34	37	10
No One Has Secure Job	3.1	12	21	25	26	16
Outstanding Performers Have Job for Life	2.5	32	22	20	20	6
Rewards Tied to Individual Performance	3.6	1	11	30	44	15
Rewards Tied to Group and/or Organization Performance	3.5	3	13	33	38	13
Loyalty to Company Rewarded	2.6	12	37	34	16	1
Rewards Tied to Seniority	1.8	47	32	14	6	1
Career Development Responsibility of Individual	3.7	1	9	26	48	15
Employees Expected to Manage Own Performance with Minimum Supervision	3.1	2	20	43	30	5
Fits Corporate Business Strategy	3.5	1	15	30	41	13
Understood by Most Employees	3.0	4	26	41	26	3
Employees Satisfied with It	2.8	6	34	40	17	3

[1]Scale of 1–5.

since all of the individuals filling out this questionnaire were senior managers, and their view of employee satisfaction may be somewhat biased. In any case, they do recognize that a significant number of employees are not necessarily satisfied with their employment contracts and perhaps would prefer to return to the more traditional one.

Finally, we asked whether a new employment contract statement was being developed. Twenty percent of the companies said that they were actively working on one, further reinforcing the impression that employment contracts are undergoing change.

Overall, the results suggest that an employment contract is in place either explicitly or implicitly that stresses that the relationship between individuals and their organizations depends on the individual's performance and, to some degree, skills. Loyalty, paternalism, and job security clearly are less important than performance.

The question of how well this new employment contract fits with total quality management, reengineering, and employee involvement is an interesting one. The strong performance emphasis in the new contract seems to fit quite well with all three of the major change initiatives that we are studying. The lack of employment security appears to fit best with reengineering, given its association with downsizing. It may fit least well with employee involvement, since some of EI practices, particularly the use of teams, require individuals to be willing to commit themselves to collective performance and collective goals. EI also requires individuals to get involved in the business at a relatively deep level. This may not be possible if people don't stay with the organization for a fairly long period of time. Individuals may also be hesitant to get involved deeply if they feel the organization is not very committed to them and their development. These issues and others concerned with how the employment contract influences the effectiveness of EI, TQM, and reengineering will be examined further in Section Twenty.

SECTION 12

Improvement Strategies

Employee involvement, total quality management, and reengineering programs are often key parts of change strategies in which other important changes may be taking place as well. In order to get a sense of the overall changes that are occurring in Fortune 1000 corporations, we asked a series of questions about improvement strategies that go beyond a focus on employee involvement, total quality management, and reengineering. Specifically, we asked about major corporate restructuring activities, the use of competencies as an important part of business strategy, and the introduction of new information and measurement technologies. All three of these activities are important in their own right and can have an impact on EI, TQM, and reengineering change efforts.

Restructuring. The desirability of a corporation focusing on a relatively limited set of businesses has its roots in Peters and Waterman's *In Search of Excellence* (1982), which strongly recommended that companies "stick to their knitting." As Table 12.1 shows, this strategy has not been the most popular approach for companies in the Fortune 1000, though there are a number of visible examples of major corporations that have adopted it, including ITT, AT&T, Rockwell, Westinghouse, and others. It is only in comparison to other kinds of changes that it is not happening frequently. Part of the explanation for this undoubtedly rests in the fact that some of the Fortune 1000 corporations have always been focused on one business, such as the public utilities and banks; thus, there is no need to change.

Only 11 percent of the companies studied are creating global business units to a very great extent. Thirty-nine percent report that they are doing it to little or no extent, which leads us to conclude that despite the attention given to the global economy, most U.S. companies are still focused on competing in the U.S. economy. In some respects, this is not surprising—quite a few of the companies in the Fortune 1000 are in service businesses and other businesses where it is difficult to create global business units. They may either be focusing primarily on the domestic market or doing a small amount of global marketing and selling; thus, they do not need to develop global business units.

Reducing the corporate staff and creating new business units are much more popular activities than is creating global business units. Over 80 percent of the companies have, to at least some extent, eliminated old units and created new ones. This is hardly surprising since for decades this type of restructuring has been part of corporate change efforts.

Table 12.1 — Percentage of Companies Using Improvement Strategies.

	Mean[1]	Little or No Extent	Some Extent	Moderate Extent	Great Extent	Very Great Extent
Reduce Number of Different Businesses	2.0	48	22	13	11	6
Create Global Business Units	2.4	39	18	14	18	11
Reduce Size of Corporate Staff	2.9	17	25	26	20	12
Restructure Corporation by Creating New Units and Eliminating Old Ones	2.9	18	27	20	24	12
Build Team-Based Organization	2.9	12	24	30	25	9
Use Temporary Project Teams to Perform Core Work	2.6	16	31	29	21	3
Focus on Core Competencies	3.4	5	21	22	36	17
Outsource Work That Is Not One of the Core Competencies or That Can Be Done More Cheaply Externally	3.0	9	24	33	23	11
Emphasize the Competencies of Employees	3.2	5	22	29	34	10
Significant Adoption of New Information Technology	3.5	7	14	24	34	21
Introduce New Performance Measures	3.3	4	22	26	34	13

[1]Scale of 1–5.

Over 80 percent of the companies have also, to at least some extent, made reductions in their corporate staff. This is a high rate of change but perhaps not a surprising one, given today's turbulent business conditions. It is also consistent with the widespread use of reengineering.

The reduction of corporate staff is particularly interesting since it is a change that can support greater employee involvement by pushing decisions downward. It also creates the possibility for many of an organization's support activities to reside closer to the individuals who are actually manufacturing products or delivering services. Thus, it fits well with the declining use of hierarchy for control purposes and with the downsizing of corporations.

We asked two questions about the use of teams as an approach to restructuring corporations. The results indicate that a large number of companies are using teams to perform core work. Eighty-eight percent report that to at least some extent they are building a team-based organization. A surprisingly high percent (84 percent) report that they are using temporary project teams to perform the core work of the organization. Here corporations seem to be responding to the need to adopt structures and put together teams that can respond quickly to the changing business environment. Overall, the results support the argument that organizations are becoming increasingly team based (Mohrman, Cohen, and Mohrman, 1995).

Competencies. Since the seminal writings on core competencies of C. K. Prahalad and Gary Hamel (see, for example, Prahalad and Hamel, 1990), the business strategy literature has paid a great deal of attention to this concept. The literature emphasizes the importance of using and developing core competencies as a key part of a business strategy.

The strategy literature argues that there are four characteristics of core competencies (Hamel, 1994; Rumelt, 1994). First, competencies represent a complex "bundle" of skills and technologies that span multiple businesses and products (for example, precision manufacturing). Second, competencies are more stable and evolve more slowly than the products and markets that have been the traditional focus of strategy. Third, core competencies are difficult to imitate. Witness the unsuccessful attempts of automakers around the world to match the productivity and quality of the Toyota production system during the past two decades. Finally, core competencies, rather than markets or products, are the true battleground for competition among firms.

The strategy literature emphasizes the importance of gaining competitive advantage through producing products and services that are related to the core competencies of an organization. For example, Sony's core competencies in miniaturization and precision manufacturing provide competitive advantages across a large number of product lines and markets.

The results in Table 12.1 strongly suggest that competencies are becoming an important part of organizational improvement strategies. Ninety-five percent of the organizations responded that at least to some extent they are focusing on core competencies in their improvement efforts. Over 50 percent report that they do this to a great or very great extent. The majority also report that to at least a moderate extent they are outsourcing work that is not related to their core competencies. Finally, the majority of the companies report that they are focusing to a moderate or greater extent on the competencies of their employees. Outsourcing and emphasizing the competencies of employees are, of course, key implementation practices if an organization wishes to focus on core competencies. Thus, they follow directly from the efforts of companies to focus on their core competencies and are a good indication that companies are using the core-competency approach to develop and implement their strategy.

Information and Measurement. Finally, the survey asked about changes in performance measures and information systems. Fifty-five percent of companies reported that to a great or very great extent, they are engaged in the significant adoption of new information technology. This is hardly surprising, given our earlier finding that reengineering programs are extremely popular. Together, these results suggest that most major U.S. corporations are going through an information revolution that is reshaping the way they gather and distribute information, manage their operations, and do business. The positive answers to the question on performance measures suggest that in many cases the changes in companies' information systems involve the use of new performance measures.

The massive changes that appear to be taking place in the use of information technology and the creation of new measures are an interesting contrast to our finding in Section Three that most employees are not getting the kind of business information that supports employee involvement. With the increased presence of information technology, it should be easy to give more and more employees the kind of business information that we considered in Section Three. Perhaps this will happen once companies further develop the new information systems and begin to realize their full power.

The results reported in this section clearly show that the changes taking place in corporations involve more than just employee involvement, total quality management, and reengineering efforts. Most corporations are changing their structures, strategies, and information systems in major ways. This is a crucial point, because it means that employee involvement, total quality management, and reengineering efforts may even be just a minor part of the changes being implemented in some organizations. This raises the important question, which we will analyze in Section Twenty-four, of how the choice of an improvement strategy is related to the adoption of EI, TQM, and reengineering, as well as the question of how these different efforts are being coordinated and managed. As our analysis of the relationship among employee involvement, total quality management, and reengineering has shown, a number of important questions exist about the sequencing of change activities and how these different activities relate to each other. Finally, given all the different types of change that are occurring, we find it hardly surprising that the employment contract, as pointed out in Section Eleven, has changed dramatically for most employees.

SECTION 13

Change Strategies

Creating change in a large corporation is more art than science. However, a growing body of literature does argue that there are certain characteristics associated with successful change efforts (see, for example, Mohrman and others, 1989; Beer, Eisenstat, and Spector, 1990; Kotter, 1997). These writings highlight the fact that organizational change is, first of all, extremely difficult to create and maintain because established patterns of behavior and established practices tend to become institutionalized and resistant to change. Even after behaviors cease to contribute to organizational effectiveness, they often continue simply because individuals are comfortable with them and because they serve them well.

Because change is difficult to initiate, the first issue that any change effort must address is "Why change?" The answer usually involves two elements to differing degrees: dissatisfaction with the status quo because it is dysfunctional, and the development of a vision that describes a new and more effective way to operate. In many cases, mobilizing a major change effort requires a combination of both dissatisfaction with the existing state and a clear vision as to what type of change is needed.

Table 13.1 presents the results from three questions that asked about the degree to which organizations have a clear vision with

| Table 13.1 | Percentage of Companies Reporting Characteristics of Change Strategy. |

Organizational Performance Improvement Efforts	Mean[1]	Little or No Extent	Some Extent	Moderate Extent	Great Extent	Very Great Extent
Guided by a Clearly Stated Business Strategy	3.4	4	19	22	40	15
Guided by Clearly Stated Beliefs About What Makes an Organization Effective	3.2	8	21	23	37	11
Guided by Mission and Values Statements	3.3	6	25	21	28	21
Driven by Threat to Organization's Survival	2.4	28	27	28	12	5

[1]Scale of 1–5.

respect to their organizational change efforts. One asked about business strategy, a second asked about beliefs concerning organizational effectiveness, and a third asked about mission and values statements. All three of these were shown to be at least moderately present in the change efforts of most of the large corporations in our study. Apparently the writing and research on organizational change has had an impact on corporations; most have made some effort to articulate their mission, strategy, and organizational effectiveness philosophy.

The final question asked whether the change effort was driven by threats to the organization's survival. Although this is true to a moderate or greater extent for almost 50 percent of the companies, it is apparently not the most powerful reason for change in many of the companies. Presumably, they are simply changing in order to improve their performance.

Table 13.2 presents the results from questions that asked about how organizational change and improvement efforts are implemented. The first four questions looked at how much integration and consistency exist across initiatives and different parts of the corporation. Most respondents reject the view that their change efforts are made up of a series of unrelated initiatives. However, a significant number—30 percent—do say that their efforts, to at least a moderate extent, could be characterized as having unrelated initiatives. In reality, this number may be quite a bit higher given the faddism that

Table 13.2	**Percentage of Companies Using Change Implementation Strategies.**					
Organizational Performance Improvement Efforts	Mean[1]	Little or No Extent	Some Extent	Moderate Extent	Great Extent	Very Great Extent
Made Up of a Series of Unrelated Initiatives	2.0	39	31	17	12	1
Integrated Company Wide	3.0	11	26	25	26	11
Occurring Differently in Different Business Units	2.9	13	24	27	30	7
Based on Bottom-Up Implementation Strategy	2.3	24	36	25	14	1
Same No Matter What Country Employees Work In	2.0	51	19	11	13	6
Led by Top Management	3.9	1	11	18	43	28
Based on Three-Year or More Plan	3.0	20	15	25	26	15

[1]Scale of 1–5.

has surrounded organizational change. In many respects, it is somewhat surprising that as many as 30 percent of senior managers would admit that their change efforts have this characteristic since it is not a desirable feature.

The next two questions asked about the degree to which change efforts are similar across business units and integrated on a company-wide basis. The answers generally indicate that they are moderately integrated company-wide; 62 percent of the respondents said that to a moderate or greater extent, the efforts are integrated company-wide. On the other hand, they also indicate that change can occur differently in different business units. In response to the question concerning the degree to which there is a bottom-up implementation strategy, only 41 percent say that such a strategy exists to a moderate or greater extent; thus, these change efforts seem closer to the approaches associated with total quality management and reengineering than to the approach associated with employee involvement, that is, they are top-down, not bottom-up, participative efforts.

There is a relatively strong trend for companies to say that their efforts are not the same from country to country. For example, 51 percent say that to little or no extent are their efforts the same from country to country.

Overall, considerable variance seems to exist in the degree to which the change efforts in corporations are similar across the board. A small number of companies apparently do allow variation by business units and use a bottom-up change process. Many others allow their change efforts to be different from country to country. Thus, many change efforts cannot be categorized as monolithic, top-down, by-the-numbers processes. Instead, they allow for some variation in how they are implemented and developed throughout large corporations. On the other hand, some corporations do report having integrated company-wide improvement efforts.

The results show that to a great extent, change efforts are led by top management. Although this doesn't necessarily mean that there is a clear vision and articulation of why change is necessary, it certainly implies that organizational improvement efforts are getting considerable attention from the top of the organization.

The final question asked about the degree to which the change effort is based on a three-year or more plan. The distribution of responses here is rather unusual. Twenty percent say this is basically not true, while 15 percent say that it is true to a very great extent. Perhaps the best way to summarize the responses is to say that companies vary tremendously in the degree to which they have long-range plans concerning their change efforts. Almost an equal number have and do not have them. Given the length of time that it may take to implement large-scale change efforts, we find it a bit surprising that more do not have a three-year or more plan. On the other hand, with the degree of change in the business environment, planning that far ahead can be a difficult and inexact exercise.

Overall, the change efforts in the Fortune 1000 are similar in some important respects. They tend to be based on a strategy and beliefs about organizational effectiveness, and they are not necessarily driven by a threat to the organization's survival. There is variance within most companies as to how change strategies are implemented, although they are likely to be led by top management. Since it seems likely that the adoption and effectiveness of EI, TQM, and reengineering efforts are in part determined by an organization's overall change strategy, these relationships will be examined in Sections Twenty and Twenty-Four.

PART FOUR

Effectiveness

Reward System Results

We asked the users of the reward system practices most commonly associated with employee involvement to rate their success in enhancing organizational performance. Table 14.1 presents the results concerning performance-based reward practices for 1990, 1993, and 1996 (these questions were not asked in the 1987 survey). Overall, the ratings for 1996 are positive and are similar to those reported in 1990 and 1993. All the pay-for-performance systems are rated as quite successful. No system was rated as unsuccessful by more than 14 percent of the companies, an impressively low rate of failure.

The highest success ratings for 1996 go to stock option and employee stock ownership plans. Profit-sharing plans are also rated as quite successful in the 1996 survey, but there is a decline in their rated effectiveness in comparison to the 1990 and 1993 surveys. The 1993 survey found that these plans had been around for over a decade. Thus, they are well established and probably not an important part of companies' current employee involvement, TQM, or performance improvement programs.

Our 1993 survey found that gainsharing was a relatively new practice in most companies, having been used for 3.2 years. Sixty-four percent rated it as either successful or very successful. The 1996 results show a lower success rating, 55 percent successful or very successful, while 9 percent rate it as unsuccessful. This is generally in line with the results of other studies that have measured the success of gainsharing (see, for example, O'Dell, 1987; U.S. General Accounting Office, 1981). They have generally found success rates of 60 to 70 percent.

Work-group or team incentives continue to be rated as quite successful. There is a relatively large percentage in the undecided category, but few report failure.

The results for nonmonetary recognition rewards are also quite favorable. Sixty-nine percent rate them as successful or very successful. In our 1993 survey, we found that these programs averaged thirteen years in use. Apparently most of them have not been introduced as part of a recent movement to improve organizational performance.

Table 14.1

Percentage of Companies Indicating Success of Performance-Based Reward Practices.

		Mean[1]	Very Unsuccessful	Unsuccessful	Undecided	Successful	Very Successful
Individual Incentives	1990	3.76	2	5	19	62	12
	1993	3.84	2	4	17	63	14
	1996	3.85	0	5	20	59	16
Work-Group or Team Incentives	1990	3.66	0	5	34	51	10
	1993	3.72	0	2	37	48	13
	1996	3.66	1	5	32	51	11
Profit Sharing	1990	3.93	0	4	25	45	26
	1993	3.99	1	3	21	44	30
	1996	3.69	2	12	19	50	17
Gainsharing	1990	3.60	1	3	43	42	12
	1993	3.72	2	5	30	47	17
	1996	3.50	1	8	36	51	4
Employee Stock Ownership Plan	1990	3.90	1	4	23	49	23
	1993	3.78	2	7	24	47	21
	1996	3.79	0	7	29	43	21
Stock Option Plan	1990	—	—	— Not Asked —		—	—
	1993	3.90	2	4	18	57	19
	1996	3.99	1	4	19	46	30
Nonmonetary Recognition Awards for Performance	1990	3.94	0	2	18	63	17
	1993	3.90	1	1	22	59	17
	1996	3.77	0	7	24	55	14

[1] Scale of 1–5

Instead, they represent well-established efforts to recognize outstanding employee performance in a wide range of areas. In some cases, of course, they may have been adapted and developed to help support an employee involvement or total quality management effort.

Table 14.2 presents the results for reward system practices that support employee involvement. Companies reporting on all-salaried pay systems indicate a 54 percent success rate. This result is lower than that found in 1990 or 1993. The reason for this decline is not clear.

| Table 14.2 | Percentage of Companies Indicating Success of Reward Practices That Support EI. |

		Mean[1]	Very Unsuccessful	Unsuccessful	Undecided	Successful	Very Successful
All-Salaried Pay Systems	1990	3.91	0	2	23	59	17
	1993	3.81	2	6	16	63	13
	1996	3.49	1	12	33	45	9
Knowledge/ Skill-Based Pay	1990	3.58	3	3	35	54	6
	1993	3.55	1	3	44	46	6
	1996	3.34	1	9	49	38	4
Flexible, Cafeteria-Style Benefits	1990	3.86	2	2	31	42	24
	1993	4.07	1	1	16	54	28
	1996	3.83	1	7	25	41	25
Employment Security	1990	—	—	— Not Asked —		—	—
	1993	3.62	3	8	26	48	15
	1996	3.19	3	13	52	28	5
Open Pay Information	1990	—	—	— Not Asked —		—	—
	1993	3.53	2	4	41	47	7
	1996	3.36	0	13	44	39	5

[1]Scale of 1–5

Our 1993 study found that most knowledge- or skill-based pay programs are relatively new (an average of four years old). Further analysis of our data shows that most of them are adopted by organizations that have recently installed self-managing teams. In 1993, 55 percent of the companies reported that their programs were a success. The success rate is lower in 1996 (42 percent). As was true in 1990 and 1993, a relatively large number of respondents in 1996 (49 percent) were undecided about the success of this practice. The slight decline in the effectiveness ratings of skill-based pay may reflect a developing sophistication concerning their advantages and disadvantages. Some plans have now been around for a number of years, and companies may be finding that they can become cumbersome and lose some of their impact.

The typical company continues to report a high success rate for its flexible benefit plan. One possible explanation for this high success rate is that considerable effort has been put into developing the technology of flexible benefits. A number of consulting firms have developed good plans; as a result, companies can implement these programs without having to do a great deal of development work on their own. They can simply outsource the design and operation of the plan to a consulting firm. Companies can thus have a high probability of success when they adopt flexible benefit programs, even though they may be doing something that is new for them.

Employment security, which has been under attack in many companies, is rated as less and less successful. It remains an open question whether some form of employment stability is needed in order to have a successful employee involvement, TQM, or any organizational change program. A number of theorists have argued that it is indeed important (see, for example, Pfeffer, 1994), but there is little or no evidence to support this assertion.

Finally, the ratings on open pay information are generally favorable (although they are somewhat less favorable than they were in 1993). Like knowledge-based pay, this category shows a high percentage of undecided respondents, but only 13 percent describe it as being unsuccessful.

The overall results reported in Tables 14.1 and 14.2 are quite positive. The respondents clearly feel that these reward system practices are important contributors to organizational performance effectiveness.

Determinants of Pay Practice Effectiveness. Our discussion of employee involvement has stressed that it is effective only if the right pattern of practices is adopted. In particular, we have argued that power and information sharing, knowledge building, and reward-oriented practices all need to be aligned. This leads to the prediction that the effectiveness of pay practices such as the ones studied in this chapter will, at least in part, depend on what information-sharing, knowledge-building, power-sharing, and other reward practices are used in combination with each of them. Generally, we would predict that they will be more effective when they are used in conjunction with practices that support employee involvement.

Table 14.3 presents the correlations between the success ratings of pay-for-performance practices and the indices of information sharing, knowledge development, power sharing, rewards, and employee involvement overall that were introduced in Section Seven. The correlations are generally positive, suggesting that the reward practices work best when they are combined with employee involvement practices in the areas of information sharing, knowledge development, and power sharing. There are two pay-for-performance practices, however, where this is not true. The first is individual incentives, whose effectiveness shows weak relationships to the use of employee involvement practices. This is not a surprising result, since individual

Table 14.3	Relationship Between Success of Pay-for-Performance Practices and Employee Involvement Indices (Correlation Coefficients).				

	Indices				
	Information	Knowledge	Rewards	Power	EI Overall
Individual Incentives	.16*	.13	.12	.12	.21**
Work-Group or Team Incentives	.17*	.20*	.08	.22**	.29***
Profit Sharing	.14	.27***	.16	.18*	.26**
Gainsharing	.03	.06	.20	–.18	–.00
Employee Stock Ownership Plan	.18*	.18*	.17	.19*	.23*
Stock Option Plan	.19*	.33***	.19*	.30***	.34***
Nonmonetary Recognition Awards for Performance	.29***	.21**	.17*	.36***	.37***

Key: * = weak relationship (p ≤ .05)
   ** = moderate relationship (p ≤ .01)
   *** = strong relationship (p ≤ .001)

incentives are not particularly thought of as being associated with employee involvement (Lawler, 1990). Much more surprising is the result for gainsharing. The previous research on gainsharing has strongly suggested that it works best when it is combined with open information and power-sharing practices (Lawler, 1990). The failure to find a positive relationship here is puzzling, since it suggests that gainsharing can be effective in the absence of these other practices.

The results for stock and nonmonetary recognition plans show a particularly strong relationship between their effectiveness and the indices of employee involvement. This is hardly surprising given that all of these plans have a relatively weak line of sight between the performance of employees and their pay. Thus, in order for these pay systems to be effective, employees need a considerable amount of information, knowledge, and power in order to create a meaningful relationship between what they do and the rewards that they receive. This result, in particular, serves to reinforce the argument that pay-for-performance plans, particularly group and organization-wide plans, work only when they are combined with supportive organizational practices, in this case, practices that are consistent with an employee involvement orientation.

Table 14.4 presents the correlations between those pay practices that are supportive of employee involvement and the indices of participation in information-sharing, knowledge development, power-sharing, rewards, and employee involvement practices. The correlations are generally positive, showing that these practices do tend to be rated as more effective when they are combined with information, knowledge, reward, and power practices that are supportive of employee involvement. However, many of the correlations are not strong, particularly the ones with knowledge- or skill-based pay, flexible benefits, and employment security.

Perhaps the most surprising result here is in relation to employment security. Pfeffer (1994) and others have argued that employment security is an important part of any employee involvement activity. The advocates of knowledge- or skill-based pay make a similar argument. Our findings do not directly contradict these arguments, but they certainly suggest that knowledge- or skill-based pay and employment security do not depend for their success on other employee involvement practices being present. In essence, their success is relatively independent of the use of other employee involvement practices.

The same is clearly not true of open pay information and all-salaried pay systems. Open pay information in particular appears to

Table 14.4

Relationship Between Success of Pay Practices and Employee Involvement Indices (Correlation Coefficients).

	Indices				
	Information	Knowledge	Rewards	Power	EI Overall
All-Salaried Pay Systems	.25**	.14	−.05	.18	.20*
Knowledge/Skill-Based Pay	.11	.22*	.06	.11	.21*
Flexible, Cafeteria-Style Benefits	.03	.15	−.05	.08	.04
Employment Security	−.23	.13	−.11	.07	.01
Open Pay Information	.25**	.16	−.16	.32***	.24**

Key: * = weak relationship (p ≤ .05)
** = moderate relationship (p ≤ .01)
*** = strong relationship (p ≤ .001)

work best when it is combined with other approaches to employee involvement. In many respects, this makes sense, since open pay information is an unusual practice and is likely to be highly disruptive in a traditional organization that does not have the ability to explain and work through the issues this practice raises. In many ways, the same may be true of all-salaried pay: it requires a certain amount of trust in order to be effective and therefore may not work particularly well in a traditional top-down organization that is not oriented toward employee involvement.

Overall, the results for the reward system practices studied are quite impressive. They receive quite favorable ratings, and these ratings as a general rule are particularly high when they are used in organizations that have adopted other employee involvement practices.

Power-
Sharing
Results

We asked the users of the power-sharing practices studied in Section Six to evaluate the success of these practices in helping improve organizational performance. Table 15.1 summarizes the results for the practices involving parallel structures. The responses for 1996 are quite similar to those obtained in 1987, 1990, and 1993. Three of the five practices are rated as successful or very successful by a majority of the respondents. The two other practices (QWL committees and suggestion systems) received more favorable than unfavorable ratings.

The most favorable ratings went to survey feedback and employee participation groups. As noted earlier, both of these approaches are parallel participation vehicles that take people out of their traditional work roles for discussions of how the workplace can be improved. These programs require no fundamental change in the management style of the organization. They are relatively easy to implement in all kinds of organizations and, as research has shown, can produce positive results in most situations (Lawler, 1986). Thus, their popularity and success are easy to understand.

Quality circles are seen as less successful than survey feedback and participation groups. This represents a significant change from 1987 when they were seen to be comparable, but it repeats the findings from 1990 and 1993. What explains these less favorable ratings? A number of articles and books have pointed out the transitory nature of their success and have warned that they may not be a good long-term approach to employee involvement (Lawler and Mohrman, 1985; Lawler, 1992). A number of companies seem to be finding that this is true. In addition, because quality circles became a fad during the 1980s, it is possible that some of the drop in their success rating is due to overuse and misuse.

Union-management quality-of-work-life (QWL) committees not only got relatively low success ratings in 1996 but they also show a significant decrease from their earlier ratings. Still, it should be noted that only 10 percent of the corporations rated them as unsuccessful. Typically, they are the most complicated parallel structure to design, implement, and manage because they must be jointly managed by unions and managements, two groups that are used to dealing with each other in a largely adversarial mode (Herrick, 1990; Bluestone and Bluestone, 1992). Furthermore, many of these structures are being established in unionized industries during difficult economic times that have brought on downsizing, layoffs, plant shutdowns, and plant consolidations. Finally, dealing in a cooperative

Table 15.1 **Percentage of Companies Indicating Success of Parallel Structure Practices.**

		Mean[1]	Very Unsuccessful	Unsuccessful	Undecided	Successful	Very Successful
Quality Circles	1987	3.79	0	5	26	55	14
	1990	3.44	1	11	36	49	4
	1993	3.46	2	11	32	48	7
	1996	3.39	4	11	34	47	4
Employee Participation Groups Other Than QCs	1987	3.85	0	3	25	57	16
	1990	3.81	1	0	26	62	11
	1993	3.88	1	1	21	66	12
	1996	3.84	0	1	25	63	11
Union-Management QWL Committees	1987	3.48	0	8	42	44	6
	1990	3.52	0	2	48	46	4
	1993	3.54	2	5	39	49	6
	1996	3.21	4	6	58	30	3
Survey Feedback	1987	3.81	1	3	27	56	14
	1990	3.72	0	5	25	60	9
	1993	3.66	1	5	35	47	13
	1996	3.69	0	9	24	58	10
Suggestion Systems	1987	—	—	— Not Asked —		—	—
	1990	—	—	— Not Asked —		—	—
	1993	3.30	3	17	34	40	7
	1996	3.19	1	21	37	38	2

[1]Scale of 1–5

problem-solving way constitutes breaking important new ground and involves developing and using new skills.

In several respects, it is becoming more and more difficult to create successful union-management programs. The continuing decline in union membership is one key factor. The leadership of the union movement seems more concerned with attracting new members in order to stem this decline than with creating cooperative programs. Companies, on the other hand, seem to feel more and more that unions are weaker and less cooperative; as a result, they may feel that they don't need to work closely with unions in order to accomplish what they need to get done.

Table 15.2 reports the results for the four work design practices: job enrichment, work teams, minibusiness units, and policy and strategy committees. These practices often require major structural changes in other design elements of the organization in order to be implemented successfully (Wellins, Byham, and Wilson, 1991; Lawler, 1992). Thus, they are more difficult to implement and operate successfully than are most of the parallel involvement practices.

The companies that report having work design programs generally say that they are successful. None of them has a failure rate of even 10 percent. In addition, they all show little change from 1987 to 1996. Particularly impressive are the success rates reported for self-managing teams and minibusiness units. Both of these approaches are relatively new, but they still have the highest percentage of very successful ratings. Apparently most of the companies that have adopted them have found them to be excellent approaches to employee involvement. This result may help explain why they are being implemented by more and more companies, and it suggests that their use will continue to increase.

All the approaches rated in Table 15.2 drew a high percentage of undecided ratings, which may reflect their newness. It may also reflect the difficulty of installing them and using them since they do require significant organizational changes. Finally, sometimes success is hard to define and measure, particularly when organizations do not collect data on the impact of their practices, as is often the case with these practices.

Overall, the high success ratings given to all the employee involvement programs that emphasize power-sharing are quite impressive. There are obviously a large number of satisfied users. This is especially significant given the newness of some of the practices and the fact that as technologies they are not well developed. Once they are

		Mean[1]	Very Unsuccessful	Unsuccessful	Undecided	Successful	Very Successful
Job Enrichment or Redesign	1987	3.55	0	4	43	46	7
	1990	3.57	0	4	40	49	7
	1993	3.52	1	2	46	48	3
	1996	3.51	0	4	45	49	3
Self-Managing Work Teams	1987	3.68	0	0	41	50	9
	1990	3.75	1	0	39	44	16
	1993	3.64	1	0	47	39	13
	1996	3.69	1	3	34	50	12
Minibusiness Units	1987	3.62	0	4	39	48	9
	1990	3.62	0	0	47	45	9
	1993	3.80	0	2	33	47	18
	1996	3.63	0	7	32	52	9
Employee Committees Concerned with Policy and/or Strategy	1987	—	—	— Not Asked —		—	—
	1990	—	—	— Not Asked —		—	—
	1993	3.58	2	1	42	50	6
	1996	3.52	2	6	39	46	8

[1]Scale of 1–5

better developed and understood, they may be seen as even more effective.

Conditions for Effectiveness. Employee involvement researchers often argue that the effectiveness of power-sharing practices, like the effectiveness of reward practices, is dependent on their being combined with an overall approach to employee involvement (Lawler, 1992, 1996). To test the degree to which the effectiveness of different power-sharing practices is related to other employee involvement practices, we correlated them. Table 15.3 presents the relationships among the suggestion involvement practices and the five indices of employee involvement introduced in Section Seven. As was expected, the overwhelming majority of the correlations are positive. The results strongly support the view that employee participation groups, survey feedback, and suggestion systems work better when they are part of an overall pattern of practices that move a company toward employee involvement.

Some interesting patterns appear in the correlations shown in Table 15.3. The effectiveness of quality circles and union-management QWL committees is not strongly associated with the presence of any of the other elements of employee involvement. In fact, union-management QWL committees are rated as less effective when they get more business information. In order to see if there were any predictors of the effectiveness of union-management QWL committees, we examined its relationship to all of the individual employee involvement practices. A significant correlation ($.31 = p \leq .01$) was found between the use of gainsharing plans and the success of union-management quality-of-work-life committees. This fits with the general argument that gainsharing plans often work well in union-management environments and can encourage labor-management cooperation (Doyle and Doyle, 1992).

Table 15.4 shows the relationships between work design practices and the indices of employee involvement. Again the results are pos-

---

Table 15.3   **Relationship Between Success of Parallel Structure Practices and EI Indices (Correlation Coefficients).**

Practice Effectiveness	Indices				
	Information	Knowledge	Rewards	Power	EI Overall
Quality Circles	−.03	.08	.05	.17	.18
Employee Participation Groups Other Than QCs	.11	.18*	.01	.31***	.18*
Union-Management QWL Committees	−.28*	−.03	.14	.11	.01
Survey Feedback	.23**	.21**	−.09	.19*	.20*
Suggestion System	.23**	.28***	−.07	.26***	.24**

Key: * = weak relationship (p ≤ .05)
  ** = moderate relationship (p ≤ .01)
  *** = strong relationship (p ≤ .001)

itive, with one exception, showing that more involvement makes most of these practices more effective. The one surprise is the result with respect to self-managing teams. They do not show the strong positive relationship that might be expected between their effectiveness and indices concerned with knowledge development, information sharing, power sharing, and reward practices. The other three power practices generally show positive practices, particularly with the measures of information sharing, knowledge development, power sharing, and the overall EI index.

It is difficult to say why there is not a stronger relationship between the effectiveness of self-managing teams and these indices. Perhaps the best explanation is that these indices measure activities on a corporate-wide basis; they do not necessarily indicate what is occurring in a particular work setting. Thus, it is quite possible that the conditions necessary for the effectiveness of self-managing work teams are present at the local level but are not related to corporate patterns of employee involvement practice adoption.

The reward index tends to show little relationship to the success of any of the four practices. Apparently, the reward practices included in this index are not particularly supportive of these approaches to power sharing. This is a surprising finding since practices such as gainsharing are generally thought to be supportive of these practices (Lawler and Cohen, 1992).

Table 15.4   **Relationship Between Success of Work Design Practices and EI Indices (Correlation Coefficients).**

Practice Effectiveness	Indices				
	Information	Knowledge	Rewards	Power	EI Overall
Job Enrichment or Redesign	.17*	.32***	–.02	.34***	.25**
Self-Managing Work Teams	.06	.11	–.03	.14	.08
Minibusiness Units	.20	.23*	–.07	.16	.14
Employee Committees Concerned with Policy and/or Strategy	.20*	.25**	.16	.22*	.31***

Key: * = weak relationship (p ≤ .05)
   ** = moderate relationship (p ≤ .01)
   *** = strong relationship (p ≤ .001)

Overall, the results show that the suggestion involvement and work design practices we studied are considered to be highly successful. The results also show, in general, that organizations that tend to adopt multiple employee involvement practices tend to have more effective power-sharing practices. The relationships are not strong, but they are consistently positive and point to the importance of systemic change.

Results of Employee Involvement Efforts

When asked, the overwhelming majority of companies respond that their employee involvement efforts are successful. This reinforces the findings reported in Sections Fourteen and Fifteen, which show that specific practices are successful. As Table 16.1 indicates, 81 percent indicate that their experience has been positive or very positive, while in 1996 only 3 percent report a negative experience. The rest (16 percent) are neutral in their assessment. This response pattern is virtually identical to the one obtained in 1993.

Organizational effectiveness can be measured in two ways: changes in internal operating processes and changes in operating results. Table 16.2 looks at the first of these. We asked companies to what extent employee involvement activities have resulted in a series of improvements in important internal operating processes and business conditions.

There is considerable variation in the degree to which these internal operations have improved. The greatest improvement is reported in four areas: participatory management, trust, management decision

Table 16.1	Experience with Employee Involvement (Percentages).		
		1993	1996
Very Negative		0	0
Negative		1	3
Neither Negative nor Positive		18	16
Positive		68	70
Very Positive		13	11

Table 16.2 — Percentage of Companies Indicating at Least Some Improvement in Internal Business Conditions as a Result of Employee Involvement.

Internal Business Conditions	1987 (n = 323)	1990 (n = 313)	1993 (n = 279)	1996 (n = 212)
Increased Employee Trust in Management	79	66	73	80
Improved Organizational Processes and Procedures	76	75	82	90
Improved Management Decision Making	74	69	76	84
Improved Employee Safety/Health	55	48	60	70
Improved Union-Management Relations	43	47	46	51
Eliminated Layers of Management or Supervision	38	50	54	51
Changed Management Style to One That Is More Participatory	79	78	83	88

Note: Companies responded 2, 3, 4, or 5 on a 5-point scale: 1 = little or no extent; 5 = very great extent; "no basis to judge" also a possible response.

making, and organizational processes and procedures. These results are generally consistent with arguments made in favor of employee involvement. They also fit with the type of employee involvement activities most frequently implemented—namely, parallel problem solving—as suggestions on how to improve operations and decision making are the most common outcome of such activities. Parallel processes can also be used to select new technologies and to make recommendations about their implementation. When management listens to and acts on these suggestions, employees' trust usually increases.

The 1996 results are generally consistent with those from 1987, 1990, and 1993. There is an overall tendency for the 1996 results to be more positive than the earlier ones, but the change is not a large one. Still, the study clearly indicates that these corporations are not becoming disillusioned with employee involvement efforts; in fact, the contrary is true.

Table 16.3 gives information about perceived changes in performance as a result of EI activities. Based on a statistical analysis, we grouped the performance measures into three types of outcomes or factors: direct performance outcomes, profitability and competitiveness, and employee satisfaction and quality of work life. As with the more global assessments of EI efforts, firms overwhelmingly report a positive experience for every outcome measured. This is true for both 1993 and 1996.

More than three-fourths of the sample report positive experiences with these outcomes. There is a small tendency for companies to perceive the strongest impact on quality of products and services, customer service, and productivity. It is noteworthy that a relatively large number of respondents (almost a fifth of the sample) indicate that they are unable to judge the impact of employee involvement efforts on profitability and competitiveness, and a relatively large percentage also perceive no impact on these outcomes. Of those reporting either a positive or negative experience, however, most rate it as positive.

Table 16.4 provides detailed information on how the adoption level of employee involvement practices is related to outcome measures, as well as to satisfaction with the overall EI effort. The results for 1993 and 1996 are quite similar. They show a strong relationship between the adoption of EI practices and the success of EI efforts. In both 1993 and 1996 the correlations for information sharing, knowledge development, and power sharing are quite high, while the correlations for rewards are low and often not significant. Overall, when it comes to getting positive results from EI efforts, more is clearly better.

Table 16.5 shows the outcome results for different EI types. The results for 1993 and 1996 are again quite similar. As might be expected, the Low Involvement companies experience the least positive results for all four outcomes. However, none of the other types holds a clear advantage; only Other Involvement gets slightly lower outcomes. All four types of firms report a very positive experience with their EI efforts on all four outcomes.

It is clear that companies that use EI practices overwhelmingly believe that they receive significant benefits from EI. The use of a wide variety of specific power-sharing, reward, information-sharing, and training practices is linked to specific positive impacts. No practice is negatively related to any outcome. Clearly corporations consistently believe that EI produces positive results and that, just as clearly, the more practices they use, the more positive are the results.

Table 16.3		Percentage of Companies Reporting EI Impacts on Performance.						
		Mean[1]	Very Negative	Negative	Neither	Positive	Very Positive	No Basis to Judge
Direct Performance Outcomes								
Productivity	1993	4.1	0	0	5	63	16	17
	1996	4.1	0	1	4	67	18	10
Quality of Products/Services	1993	4.2	0	0	4	62	20	14
	1996	4.2	0	1	6	61	24	9
Customer Service	1993	4.2	0	0	6	56	22	15
	1996	4.3	0	1	7	51	32	10
Speed of Response	1993	4.0	0	0	10	59	13	18
	1996	3.7	0	3	28	41	6	22
Profitability and Competitiveness								
Competitiveness	1993	3.9	0	0	14	57	7	22
	1996	4.0	0	0	17	53	13	17
Profitability	1993	3.9	0	0	19	51	8	22
	1996	4.0	0	1	15	51	15	19
Employee Satisfaction and QWL								
Employee Satisfaction	1993	4.0	0	2	13	59	12	15
	1996	4.1	0	0	10	59	19	13
Employee Quality of Work Life	1993	3.9	0	1	15	58	7	19
	1996	4.0	0	1	14	58	12	15

[1]Scale of 1–5. Mean score calculated with No Basis to Judge = missing.

Table 16.4

Relationship Between Extent of Adoption of EI Practices and EI Outcomes (Significant Correlation Coefficients).

EI Practice	Direct Performance Outcomes✪		Profitability and Competitiveness		Employee Satisfaction and QWL		Satisfaction with EI Overall	
	1993	1996	1993	1996	1993	1996	1993	1996
Information (Index)	.29***	.22**	.27***	.23**	.14*	.21**	.23***	.17*
Corporation's operating results	.18**		.17*			.19*	.18**	
Unit's operating results	.28***	.20*	.20**	.23**		.17*	.15*	.26***
New technologies	.15*	.27***		.23**		.22**	.14*	
Business plans/goals	.22***		.22***				.12*	
Competitors' performance	.25***		.28***	.23**	.13*		.28***	
Knowledge (Index)	.31***	.44***	.31***	.38***	.21**	.20**	.31***	.26***
Group decision-making/ problem-solving skills	.27***	.25**	.22***	.33***	.18**	.28***	.28***	.21**
Leadership skills	.19**	.19*	.26***	.23**	.13*		.21***	.16*
Skills in understanding the business	.13*	.25**	.23***	.27***	.13*		.14*	.20**
Quality/statistical analysis skills	.25***	.39***	.27***	.29***	.18**	.28***	.28***	.19**
Team-building skills	.19**	.26***	.21**	.19*		.18*	.26***	.21**
Job-skills training	.15*	.27***		.18*			.22***	.17*
Cross-training	.29***	.36***	.16*	.22**	.16*		.18**	.15*
Rewards (Index)	.17**		.13*				.24***	
All-salaried pay systems								
Knowledge-/skill-based pay			.15*	.20*			.16**	.19**
Profit sharing	.17**		.20**					
Gainsharing							.18**	
Individual incentives			.14*				.18**	
Work group/team incentives							.12*	
Nonmonetary recognition awards	.14*						.26***	
Employee stock ownership plans	.13*	.18*					.19**	
Flexible, cafeteria-style benefits								
Employment security	.17**	.19*	.26***		.20**		.21***	
Open pay information		.23**	.19**	.17*		.16*		.19**
Stock option plan							.12*	

✪ (Productivity, customer satisfaction, quality, and speed)
Key: * = weak relationship (p ≤ .05)
　　** = moderate relationship (p ≤ .01)
　　*** = strong relationship (p ≤ .001)

Table 16.4 (Continued)

EI Practice	Direct Performance Outcomes❂		Profitability and Competitiveness		Employee Satisfaction and QWL		Satisfaction with EI Overall	
	1993	1996	1993	1996	1993	1996	1993	1996
Power (Index)	.22***	.40***	.23***	.37***	.23***	.19*	.39***	.40***
Suggestion system	.20**	.26**		.25**			.22***	.23***
Survey feedback				.22***			.25***	
Job enrichment or redesign	.21***	.34***		.32***		.15*	.24***	.34***
Quality circles		.29***		.20*		.20**	.23***	.19**
Employee participation groups	.24***	.39***		.24**			.29***	.34***
Union-management QWL committees							.17**	.21**
Minibusiness units	.17*	.20*		.23**			.18**	.20**
Self-managing work teams	.15*						.27***	.26***
Employee policy/ strategy committees	.25***						.27***	

Key: * = weak relationship (p ≤ .05)
    ** = moderate relationship (p ≤ .01)
    *** = strong relationship (p ≤ .001)

Table 16.5   **Mean EI Outcome Scores by EI Types.**

EI Type		Direct Performance Outcomes❂	Profitability and Competitiveness	Employee Satisfaction and QWL	Satisfaction with EI Overall
Low involvement	1993	3.9	3.6	3.7	3.7
	1996	3.9	3.7	4.0	3.6
Suggestion involvement	1993	4.2	4.0	4.0	4.0
	1996	4.2	4.1	4.0	3.9
Job involvement	1993	4.3	4.3	4.0	4.0
	1996	4.3	4.2	4.2	4.3
Business involvement	1993	4.2	4.0	4.2	4.1
	1996	4.1	4.2	4.2	4.4
Other involvement	1993	4.2	4.0	3.9	4.0
	1996	4.1	3.8	3.8	3.9

❂ (Productivity, customer satisfaction, quality, and speed)
Note: All outcomes are measured on a 5-point response scale.

Results of TQM Efforts

Seventy-six percent of those companies with TQM programs report that their experience with them has been positive or very positive (see Table 17.1). This finding is somewhat lower than the result obtained in 1993 when 83 percent reported positive or very positive experiences. Although we should not overinterpret this relatively small decrease in satisfaction, still it may indicate a slight decline in the perceived effectiveness of TQM programs. It also means that TQM programs now have a slightly lower rating than employee involvement programs (76 percent versus 81 percent, respectively).

Table 17.2 shows the perception of the impact of TQM programs on a number of organizational effectiveness outcomes. For both 1993 and 1996, the results are quite positive. On virtually all of the ratings, at least two-thirds of the respondents indicate that the impact of TQM has been positive, with almost no companies feeling that there have been negative effects.

A significant number of respondents do report that they could not judge the outcomes, perhaps because it was too early to tell. Another small group felt that the impact of TQM is neutral on particular outcomes. It is also worth noting that the results are slightly lower for the two employee outcome items.

The outcomes in Table 17.2 are clustered into the same three outcome groupings, or factors, reported in Section Sixteen. These groupings are highly correlated with one another, as well as with the overall rating of satisfaction with TQM. The first factor reflects the work performance outcomes that employee behavior can directly impact: productivity, quality of products and services, customer service, and speed. In both 1993 and 1996, corporations perceive TQM's impact to be slightly higher for these outcomes than for the other groupings. The second factor contains overall company performance outcomes: profitability and competitiveness. The third factor consists of the employee outcomes: satisfaction and quality of work life. Although clearly in the positive range, companies are experiencing slightly less impact in these last outcomes than in the direct work performance arena. This pattern resembles that found for EI programs, though the results for employee satisfaction are slightly higher for EI.

Table 17.3 shows how the use of specific TQM practices relates to the three kinds of outcomes and to overall satisfaction with TQM. The use of core TQM practices is strongly related to direct work performance outcomes, company performance, and satisfaction

Table 17.1	Experience with Total Quality Management (Percentages).	
	1993	1996
Very Negative	0	0
Negative	1	4
Neither Negative nor Positive	16	20
Positive	66	70
Very Positive	17	6

with TQM. It is less strongly related to employee outcomes. The use of production-oriented TQM practices is linked most strongly to direct and company outcomes and to satisfaction with TQM. It is not significantly related to employee outcomes.

The use of the two individual TQM practices, cost-of-quality monitoring and collaboration with suppliers, is related to company performance, direct performance, and satisfaction with TQM in both 1993 and 1996 but not to employee outcomes. This is not surprising, since when these two practices are implemented, they are often oriented directly to performance improvement.

We also examined whether the percent of employees covered by TQM efforts relates to the outcomes. The results in Table 17.3 show that the three outcomes and the company's overall satisfaction with TQM are all higher when a greater percentage of employees are covered.

The general pattern of relationships shows that TQM is successful and is contributing to company outcomes. This finding is supported by the favorable rating of TQM programs and by the finding that the amount of coverage by TQM practices is strongly related to company performance. In addition, there is a strong relationship between core and production-oriented practices and two measures of performance: direct performance outcomes and profitability. However, there are few significant relationships with employee outcomes, suggesting that widespread adoption of TQM does not necessarily mean a more satisfying work situation for employees.

Table 17.2 Percentage of Companies Reporting Impacts of TQM.

		Mean[1]	Very Negative	Negative	Neither	Positive	Very Positive	No Basis to Judge
Direct Performance Outcomes								
Productivity	1993	4.0	0	1	11	66	14	9
	1996	4.0	0	0	14	60	17	9
Quality of Product/Services	1993	4.2	0	0	3	69	20	7
	1996	4.2	0	0	5	61	27	7
Customer Service	1993	4.2	0	0	3	70	20	8
	1996	4.2	0	0	6	61	28	5
Speed of Response	1993	4.0	0	0	9	68	11	12
	1996	3.7	0	2	33	43	7	15
Profitability and Competitiveness								
Competitiveness	1993	4.0	0	0	9	68	9	14
	1996	4.1	0	0	7	66	14	13
Profitability	1993	3.9	0	0	19	53	10	17
	1996	4.0	0	0	15	63	10	12
Employee Satisfaction and QWL								
Employee Satisfaction	1993	3.8	0	1	19	61	6	13
	1996	3.8	0	2	19	60	7	12
Employee Quality of Work Life	1993	3.8	0	1	21	56	7	16
	1996	3.7	1	2	23	54	3	18

[1] Scale of 1–5. Mean score calculated with No Basis to Judge = missing.

Table 17.3 **Relationship of TQM Outcomes to Extent of Adoption of TQM Practices (Significant Correlation Coefficients).**

	Perceived TQM Outcomes							
	Direct Performance Outcomes✪		Profitability and Competitiveness		Employee Satisfaction and QWL		Satisfaction with TQM Overall	
	1993	1996	1993	1996	1993	1996	1993	1996
Core Practices Overall	.31***	.47***	.35***	.38***	.25***	.22*	.39***	.34***
Quality Improvement Teams	.27***	.41***	.34***	.36***	.30***		.38***	.42***
Quality Councils	.19**	.24*	.18*	.21*	.18*		.32***	
Cross-Functional Planning	.23***	.35***	.31***	.33***	.21**		.25***	.28**
Work Simplification	.23***	.37***	.27***	.30***			.31***	.27**
Customer Satisfaction Monitoring	.28***	.34***	.27***	.24**	.16*		.26***	.21*
Direct Employee Exposure to Customers	.24***	.23*	.25***		.20**		.30***	
Production-Oriented Practices Overall	.23***	.38***	.27***	.40***			.31***	.31***
Self-Inspection	.20**	.34***	.24***	.36***			.22**	.22*
Statistical Control Method Used by Front-Line Employees	.23***	.28**	.25***	.33***			.30***	.39***
Just-in-Time Deliveries	.17*	.31**	.21**		.16*		.27***	
Work Cells or Manufacturing Cells	.15*	.36***	.16*	.41***			.18*	.28**
Other Practices								
Cost-of-Quality Monitoring	.15*	.29**	.22**	.39***			.25***	.35***
Collaboration with Suppliers in Quality Efforts	.16*	.34***	.21**	.28**			.25***	.23**
Percent Employees Involved	.27***	.37***	.29***	.27**	.23**	.19*	.37***	.39***

✪ (Productivity, customer satisfaction, quality, and speed)
Key: * = weak relationship (p ≤ .05)
   ** = moderate relationship (p ≤ .01)
   *** = strong relationship (p ≤ .001)

Process Reengineering Results

Reengineering became a widely used approach to improving organizational effectiveness during the 1990s, as the results presented in Section Nine clearly show. Perhaps because of its popularity, it is often accused of being faddish and potentially damaging to companies and individuals. Even though it is frequently criticized, little objective data exist that demonstrate the effectiveness of reengineering programs.

The few studies that have been done on reengineering have tended to ask questions such as whether reengineering programs "live up to their promise." In general, these studies have shown relatively negative results, with the majority of respondents reporting that reengineering efforts have not lived up to their promises. Since reengineering programs are usually conducted by consulting firms, this may well mean that reengineering efforts do not deliver the results that consulting firms have promised when they sold corporations on the idea.

We asked the Fortune 1000 companies how positive or negative was their experience with process reengineering efforts. We asked the question in this way in order to measure whether corporations felt that reengineering efforts were worth undertaking or not. Asking whether an effort has lived up to its promise is less likely to elicit this information. It is quite possible for a program to fall short of expectations but still be an experience that is more positive than negative and one that is worth undertaking.

The results in Table 18.1 show that reengineering projects are in fact viewed positively. Only 7 percent of the companies say that

Table 18.1	Experience With Process Reengineering Efforts (Percentages).
	1996
Very Negative	1
Negative	6
Neither Negative nor Positive	28
Positive	61
Very Positive	5

their experience was negative, while 66 percent say that it was either positive or very positive. This is a high endorsement level, though it is lower than the ratings obtained for TQM (76 percent) and employee involvement programs (81 percent). The data raise an interesting question: What is the basis for all of the criticism that abounds about work process reengineering?

Table 18.2 helps to establish the relative strengths and weaknesses of process reengineering efforts. The employee satisfaction and QWL items tend to show neutral to slightly negative results. Thus, unlike EI and TQM efforts, reengineering efforts often do not have a positive impact and in about 20 percent of the cases have a negative impact on the human side of the enterprise.

The results for the direct performance outcomes and the profitability and competitiveness outcomes are strikingly different from those for the human resources outcomes; they are overwhelmingly positive. For example, 79 percent of the respondents report positive results in the area of productivity. The quality of products and services is seen to

Table 18.2 **Percentage of Companies Reporting Process Reengineering Impacts .**

	Mean[1]	Very Negative	Negative	Neither	Positive	Very Positive	No Basis to Judge
Direct Performance Outcomes							
Productivity	4.0	0	2	11	68	11	9
Quality of Product/Services	3.8	1	1	22	58	10	10
Customer Service	3.9	0	2	19	56	15	8
Speed of Response	3.9	0	3	21	50	16	11
Profitability and Competitiveness							
Competitiveness	4.0	0	1	13	63	12	12
Profitability	4.0	0	1	15	58	16	9
Employee Satisfaction and QWL							
Worker Satisfaction	3.2	1	20	36	32	1	11
Employee Quality of Work Life	3.1	1	17	39	23	3	18

[1] Scale of 1–5. Mean score calculated with No Basis to Judge = missing.

increase by 68 percent of the respondents. Profitability is seen to increase by 74 percent of the respondents. Finally, 66 percent perceive increases in speed; seventy-five percent of the respondents feel competitiveness has improved. Overall, the results show a mixed impact for process reengineering: a very positive impact on operational results competitiveness and profitability and a much less positive impact on employees.

Table 18.3 shows the relationship between the adoption rate of reengineering practices and the outcomes from reengineering. The work-restructuring practices all show strong relationships to the direct performance outcomes and to profitability and competitiveness. They are also quite strongly related to satisfaction with the reengineering effort overall. Their relationships to employee satisfaction and quality of work life are significant but slightly lower. Overall, the work-restructuring practices show a strong relationship to the outcomes of reengineering efforts. They appear to contribute positively to both employee outcomes and organizational effectiveness. Greater use of them results in significantly more positive outcomes.

The cost reduction practices associated with reengineering show generally positive relationships to the direct performance outcomes and to profitability and competitiveness. They show a somewhat lower but still significant relationship to satisfaction with the reengineering effort overall. The lower correlation with the overall satisfaction rating may well reflect the lack of a significant relationship between the adoption of these practices and employee satisfaction and quality work life. It is clear from the lack of significant correlations between the cost reduction practices and employee satisfaction and quality of work life that doing more (or even the same) with fewer people or less supervision is not associated with positive outcomes for employees.

The results showing the relationship between the percent of employees covered and the outcomes of reengineering are similar to those found for cost reduction. Covering a greater percentage of the employees contributes positively to direct performance outcomes and profitability and competitiveness but not to employee satisfaction and quality of work life. Overall these results are consistent with the general impact of reengineering reported in Table 18.2. Reengineering has many benefits for the performance of organizations, but its impact on employees is not necessarily positive.

Given these results, we find it hardly surprising that reengineering is both popular and controversial. An organizational change effort that corporations view as producing very positive results for company performance but as having a negative or neutral impact on

Table 18.3 **Relationship Between Extent of Adoption of Reengineering Practices and Reengineering Outcomes (Correlation Coefficients).**

Reengineering Practice	Direct Performance Outcomes✪	Profitability and Competitiveness	Employee Satisfaction and QWL	Satisfaction with Reengineering Overall
Work Restructuring Overall	.58***	.52***	.34***	.48***
Process simplification	.58***	.42***	.27**	.49***
Creation of cross-functional units (such as departments or customer- or product-focused units)	.43***	.42***	.29***	.38***
Major information system redesign	.38***	.30***	.19*	.24**
Enriched multiskilled individual jobs	.43***	.31***	.26**	.35***
Multiskilled teams	.45***	.40***	.32***	.38***
Cost Reduction Overall	.31***	.43***	.05	.27***
Doing the same work with fewer people	.29***	.34***	−.04	.16*
Doing the same work with less supervision	.21*	.34***	.04	.22**
A lower overall cost structure	.33***	.45***	.13	.33***
Percent Covered	.23**	.24**	.11	.19*

✪ (Productivity, customer satisfaction, quality, and speed)
Key: * = weak relationship (p ≤ .05)
    ** = moderate relationship (p ≤ .01)
    *** = strong relationship (p ≤ .001)

employees is bound to be controversial. Indeed, our results may understate the seriousness of reengineering's negative impact on employees, since we received our answers from senior managers in the corporations, and they may not be as aware of all the negative human resource impacts of reengineering as are employees at lower levels in the organization. If we had talked to the rank-and-file employees in these companies, we may well have gotten much more negative ratings for reengineering. On the other hand, the data did frequently come from human resource executives who ought to have at least some awareness of how the practices are impacting most of a firm's employees.

The data raise the question of whether a change program that has a negative or neutral impact on the human resources side of an organization can sustain the positive results that it appears to offer in operational areas. In areas such as customer service, we must ask whether more dissatisfied employees can and will, over the long term, deliver improved service (see, for example, Schneider and Bowen, 1995).

A second question raised by these somewhat mixed results is whether reengineering's popularity will continue to grow. A good guess is that it probably will not—at least with respect to cost reduction—because potential customers are increasingly aware of the negative outcomes associated with it. But perhaps more important, most organizations have already had one experience with reengineering; thus, they are now directly aware of the negative outcomes. This may make them highly resistant to new attempts to sell them reengineering programs; indeed, reengineering may well turn out to be something that organizations become inoculated against after one experience.

SECTION 19

Combining Employee Involvement, Total Quality Management, and Reengineering

Employee involvement, total quality management, and process reengineering have both similarities and important differences. The most important were highlighted in Section One. The results presented up to this point clearly show that many companies often adopt more than one program or set of practices. This raises important questions about how joint adoption influences the effectiveness of each one.

Employee Involvement and Total Quality Management. We pointed out in Section One that although both TQM and EI stress employee involvement as well as training and skills development, there are also some key differences between them. The TQM literature attends more to work process and customer outcomes. The employee involvement literature emphasizes design of the work and business units for fuller business involvement and employee motivation. In addition, employee involvement emphasizes making the employee a stakeholder in business performance. In practice, these two management approaches may contribute to organizational effectiveness in a complementary and reinforcing way so that the absence of one weakens the impact of the other.

Table 19.1 shows the correlations between the use of TQM practices and the company's perceived outcomes from its EI activities.

Table 19.1

Relationship of EI Outcomes to TQM Use (Correlation Coefficients).

	EI Outcomes							
	Direct Performance Outcomes○		Profitability and Competitiveness		Employee Satisfaction and QWL		Satisfaction with EI Overall	
TQM Indices	1993	1996	1993	1996	1993	1996	1993	1996
Core TQM Practices	.28***	.36***	.27***	.27**	.15*	.07	.33***	.29***
Production-Oriented Practices	.39***	.40***	.26***	.29**	.29***	.16	.21**	.32***

○ (Productivity, customer satisfaction, quality, and speed)
Key:　* = weak relationship (p ≤ .05)
　　　** = moderate relationship (p ≤ .01)
　　　*** = strong relationship (p ≤ .001)

The use of the core TQM practices is related to the performance and company outcomes of EI in both 1993 and 1996. It is not related to the employee outcomes from EI. The use of the production-oriented TQM practices relates to all three kinds of EI outcomes in 1993, but it does not relate to employee outcomes in 1996. Both the core and the production practices are related to satisfaction with the impact of EI. Overall, the results suggest that the more organizations use TQM practices, the more positive results they get from their EI efforts, particularly with respect to organizational performance outcomes. TQM appears to help EI programs have a stronger impact on organizational performance.

Table 19.2 shows that most of the indices of employee involvement are related to the TQM outcomes, especially to company outcomes. Power sharing, an emphasis shared by TQM and EI, is most strongly related to the employee outcomes of TQM. Rewards, in contrast, are not related to the outcomes of TQM. Overall, the results suggest that the more organizations use EI practices, the more likely they are to have successful TQM programs.

These findings regarding the impact of TQM and EI are not unexpected: most TQM proponents advocate high levels of employee involvement as a part of their TQM efforts. However, the data do make an important point: the impact of TQM programs that do not include EI practices will be less positive both for employee outcomes and for performance outcomes.

The findings presented in Section Ten showed that companies using the most advanced form of EI, business involvement, are the greatest

Table 19.2   **Relationship of TQM Outcomes to EI Use (Correlation Coefficients).**

| | TQM Outcomes | | | | | | | |
| | Direct Performance Outcomes✪ | | Profitability and Competitiveness | | Employee Satisfaction and QWL | | Satisfaction with TQM Overall | |
Employee Involvement Indices	1993	1996	1993	1996	1993	1996	1993	1996
EI Overall	.21**	.45***	.29***	.38***	.19*	.24*	.25***	.15
Information	.20**	.34***	.20**	.31***	.13	.24*	.14	.04
Knowledge and Skills	.17*	.40***	.31***	.42***	.20**	.17	.27***	.21*
Rewards	.11	.19	.10	.19	–.01	.01	.10	–.03
Power Sharing	.22**	.37***	.33***	.37***	.25***	.26**	.23***	.37***

✪ (Productivity, customer satisfaction, quality, and speed)
Key: * = weak relationship (p ≤ .05)
     ** = moderate relationship (p ≤ .01)
    *** = strong relationship (p ≤ .001)

users of most TQM practices. Table 19.3 demonstrates that these companies also experience the greatest impact of TQM on profitability and competitiveness and (in 1993) on employee satisfaction and QWL. Companies employing job involvement approaches report slightly higher impact of TQM on direct work performance outcomes (1993 only), although the differences between the suggestion, job, and business involvement companies are not statistically significant for this outcome. Overall, the data clearly suggest that any of the three types of involvement lead to more effective TQM programs than does low involvement.

Table 19.4 shows, for 1996, that the sequence in which TQM and EI are implemented is not strongly or consistently related to their impact on direct performance, company outcomes, or employee outcomes. Overall, there seems to be little difference in either EI or TQM outcomes based on which program started first.

Particularly in 1993, the employee outcomes from TQM and the company outcomes from EI are highest when the two initiatives are managed in an integrated fashion (see Table 19.5). Coordination helps, but both employee and company outcomes tend to be slightly higher if the two efforts are integrated.

Table 19.3

Relationship of TQM Outcomes to EI Type.

| | TQM Outcomes | | | | | | | |
| | Direct Performance Outcomes✪ | | Profitability and Competitiveness | | Employee Satisfaction and QWL | | Satisfaction with TQM Overall | |
EI Type	1993	1996	1993	1996	1993	1996	1993	1996
Low EI	3.93	3.82	3.71	3.84	3.65	3.67	3.75	3.50
Suggestion Involvement	4.16	4.20	4.00	4.12	3.87	3.87	4.15	4.06
Job Involvement	4.24	4.13	4.17	4.16	3.75	3.88	4.00	3.95
Business Involvement	4.15	4.11	4.25	4.28	4.00	3.81	4.36	3.90
Other	4.10	4.11	4.00	4.07	3.84	3.50	3.88	3.50

✪ (Productivity, customer satisfaction, quality, and speed)
Note: Means are reported; scale of 1–5.

Table 19.4

Relationship of TQM and EI Outcomes to When EI and TQM Started.

| | | EI Started First | | Simultaneous | | TQM Started First | |
		1993	1996	1993	1996	1993	1996
Direct Performance Outcomes✪	EI	4.15	4.16	4.19	4.12	4.16	4.07
	TQM	4.12	4.03	4.16	4.17	4.05	3.96
Profitability and Competitiveness	EI	3.97	4.04	3.99	3.90	3.84	4.14
	TQM	3.93	4.00	4.05	4.07	3.88	3.99
Employee Satisfaction and QWL	EI	4.06*	4.13	3.95	4.02	3.87	4.19
	TQM	3.86*	3.73	4.00*	3.84	3.70	3.72

✪ (Productivity, customer satisfaction, quality, and speed)
Note: Means are presented and compared (scale of 1–5).
* = Significantly higher than the unstarred time relationship.

Table 19.5   Relationship of TQM Outcomes to How EI and TQM Are Managed.

		Two Separate Programs		Coordinated		One Integrated Program	
		1993	1996	1993	1996	1993	1996
Direct Performance Outcomes✪	EI	4.04	4.05	4.20	4.19	4.21	4.13
	TQM	4.02	3.94	4.09	4.01	4.14	4.13
Profitability and Competitiveness	EI	3.77	3.94	3.90	3.96	4.00*	4.11
	TQM	3.85	3.98	3.96	3.89	3.97	4.09
Employee Satisfaction and QWL	EI	3.92	4.06	3.98	4.17	3.96	4.12
	TQM	3.70	3.69	3.76	3.83	3.90*	3.77

✪ (Productivity, customer satisfaction, quality, and speed)
Note: Means are presented and compared (scale of 1–5).
* = Significantly higher than the unstarred time relationship.

The 1993 data in Table 19.6 show a trend for direct performance outcomes from both TQM and EI ,and the company outcomes from EI to be higher when EI is seen as an important part of TQM rather than the reverse. This result, however, is not replicated in the 1996 data; thus, strong support is lacking for choosing among these alternatives.

Reengineering Effectiveness. Reengineering is most closely linked in its concepts and practices to TQM. Both emphasize lateral processes and a significant restructuring of work content. The relationship between employee involvement and reengineering is less direct, and some think that reengineering is an impediment to employee involvement. Reengineering does not, for example, include an emphasis on employee involvement, and as we noted in Section One, it is often implemented in a relatively top-down manner. With the differences between employee involvement and reengineering, it is an open question as to how the presence of employee involvement practices will impact the effectiveness of reengineering.

Table 19.7 shows that the presence of employee involvement practices is associated with more positive outcomes from reengineering efforts. Power sharing as an employee involvement practice in particular tends to be associated with all four of the outcome measures

Table 19.6

Relationship of How EI and TQM Are Perceived to EI and TQM Outcomes.

		EI Is an Important Part of TQM		TQM Is an Important Part of EI	
		1993	1996	1993	1996
Direct Performance Outcomes✪	EI	4.20*	4.13	3.98	4.08
	TQM	4.14*	4.09	3.95	3.99
Profitability and Competitiveness	EI	3.95*	4.03	3.73	4.05
	TQM	3.97	4.07	3.80	3.94
Employee Satisfaction and QWL	EI	3.97	4.08	3.90	4.16
	TQM	3.86	3.76	3.67	3.78

✪ (Productivity, customer satisfaction, quality, and speed)
Note: Means are presented and compared.
* = Significantly higher than the unstarred time relationship.

Table 19.7

Relationship of Reengineering Outcomes to Use of Employee Involvement (Correlation Coefficients).

Employee Involvement Indices	Reengineering Outcomes			
	Direct Performance Outcomes✪	Profitability and Competitiveness	Employee Satisfaction and QWL	Satisfaction with Reengineering Overall
EI Overall	.27**	.26**	.21*	.13
Information	.18*	.12	.02	.04
Knowledge and Skills	.24**	.22**	.28***	.16*
Rewards	.08	.11	.08	−.03
Power Sharing	.25**	.29***	.26**	.22**

✪ (Productivity, customer satisfaction, quality, and speed)
Key: * = weak relationship (p ≤ .05)
   ** = moderate relationship (p ≤ .01)
   *** = strong relationship (p ≤ .001)

of reengineering programs. Although these relationships are not exceptionally strong, they do indicate that to some degree, EI practices can improve the effectiveness of reengineering programs. This may well come about because EI deals with some of the employee issues that many reengineering programs neglect. Thus, the EI activities may help improve the impact of reengineering programs on employees and organizational effectiveness.

Table 19.8 looks at the relationship between reengineering outcomes and the use of TQM. As we expected, there are consistent positive relationships between the use of TQM practices and the effectiveness of reengineering programs. This is particularly true when the focus is on reengineering's direct performance outcomes and its profitability and competitiveness outcomes. There is no relationship between the adoption of TQM practices and the impact of reengineering on employee satisfaction and quality of work life. This, too, is hardly surprising. TQM, like reengineering, tends not to place as much emphasis on employee outcomes, so the two approaches do not compensate for each other in this area.

Overall, the results suggest that both employee involvement and TQM practices can help reengineering programs be more successful. In the area of organizational outcomes, this is particularly true of total quality management practices. With respect to employee outcomes, employee involvement practices can help reengineering have more positive outcomes. They can also have some effect on the organizational outcomes of a reengineering effort.

The outcomes of employee involvement programs are significantly correlated with the use of reengineering practices. As shown in Table 19.9, the work structure and cost reduction practices relate to three of the four employee involvement outcome measures. Not surprisingly, employee satisfaction is unrelated to the use of reengineering practices. What is unexpected are the consistently strong correlations between all of the work structure and cost reduction items and the three outcomes of employee involvement programs that are concerned with organizational performance. A possible explanation for these strong relationships is that reengineering brings to EI programs a stronger orientation toward performance and the bottom line, as well as practices that are particularly targeted at producing improvements in organizational performance. Thus, reengineering serves to facilitate the organizational impact of an EI program.

Table 19.10 shows the relationship between the TQM outcomes and the use of reengineering. These are consistently positive for

TQM Practices	Reengineering Outcomes			
	Direct Performance Outcomes✪	Profitability and Competitiveness	Employee Satisfaction and QWL	Satisfaction with Reengineering Overall
Core Practices Overall	.33**	.41***	–.01	.17
Quality Improvement Teams	.23*	.32***	.05	.21*
Quality Councils	.02	.16	–.23*	–.01
Cross-Functional Planning	.33***	.39***	.08	.20*
Work Simplification	.33**	.43***	.12	.21*
Customer Satisfaction Monitoring	.33***	.34***	–.07	.12
Direct Employee Exposure to Customers	.09	.12	–.06	–.05
Production-Oriented Practices Overall	.33**	.37***	.23*	.15
Self-Inspection	.26*	.30**	.13	.13
Statistical Control Method Used by Front-Line Employees	.25*	.28**	.08	.19*
Just-in-Time Deliveries	.25*	.25*	.05	.12
Work Cells or Manufacturing Cells	.25*	.26*	.21	.14
Other Practices				
Cost-of-Quality Monitoring	.16	.32**	.01	.22*
Collaboration with Suppliers in Quality Efforts	.26*	.36***	–.04	.18

✪ (Productivity, customer satisfaction, quality, and speed)
Key: * = weak relationship (p ≤ .05)
    ** = moderate relationship (p ≤ .01)
    *** = strong relationship (p ≤ .001)

Table 19.9

Relationship of Employee Involvement Outcomes to Reengineering Use (Correlation Coefficients).

Reengineering Practices	EI Outcomes			
	Direct Performance Outcomes✪	Profitability and Competitiveness	Employee Satisfaction and QWL	Satisfaction with EI Overall
Work Structure	.37***	.31***	.09	.37***
Process Simplification	.29***	.21*	−.02	.26***
Creation of Cross-Functional Units	.27**	.27**	.12	.24**
Major Information System Redesign	.22*	.22*	.10	.21**
Enriched Multiskilled Individual Jobs	.29***	.27**	.03	.27***
Multiskilled Teams	.34***	.24**	.11	.44***
Cost Reduction	.35***	.34***	.03	.29***
Doing Same Work with Fewer People	.36***	.26**	.03	.20**
Doing Same Work with Less Supervision	.32***	.30***	.02	.29***
Lower Overall Cost Structure	.26**	.36***	.03	.28***

✪ (Productivity, customer satisfaction, quality, and speed)
Key: * = weak relationship (p ≤ .05)
    ** = moderate relationship (p ≤ .01)
    *** = strong relationship (p ≤ .001)

three of the four possible outcome areas. Not surprisingly, employee satisfaction is not related to the use of reengineering practices. The three other outcome measures, however, are generally related to the use of reengineering practices. This result is not unexpected given the complementarity of the change activities that are involved in reengineering and total quality management. As noted in Section One, both tend to emphasize taking a process orientation, and in many cases both result in the ability to reduce the number of employees in an organization.

Overall, the results suggest that reengineering can help both employee involvement and total quality management be more effective with respect to performance, profitability, and overall program

Table 19.10 — Relationship of Total Quality Management Outcomes to Reengineering Use (Correlation Coefficients).

Reengineering Practices	TQM Outcomes			
	Direct Performance Outcomes✪	Profitability and Competitiveness	Employee Satisfaction and QWL	Satisfaction with TQM Overall
Work Structure	.34***	.39***	−.01	.22*
Process Simplification	.33***	.33***	.04	.26**
Creation of Cross-Functional Units	.30**	.32**	.01	.17
Major Information System Redesign	.22*	.15	−.11	.09
Enriched Multiskilled Individual Jobs	.17	.30**	−.07	.11
Multiskilled Teams	.27**	.43***	.12	.25**
Cost Reduction	.26*	.36***	.03	.29**
Doing Same Work with Fewer People	.32**	.33***	.10	.33***
Doing Same Work with Less Supervision	.16	.32***	.04	.28**
Lower Overall Cost Structure	.23*	.33***	−.05	.19*

✪ (Productivity, customer satisfaction, quality, and speed)
Key: * = weak relationship (p ≤ .05)
  ** = moderate relationship (p ≤ .01)
  *** = strong relationship (p ≤ .001)

effectiveness. The use of reengineering does not help total quality management or employee involvement have more positive impacts on employee satisfaction. From a performance point of view, then, the evidence presented in Tables 19.9 and 19.10 provides further support for the argument that there is a certain complementarity among employee involvement, total quality management, and reengineering.

Table 19.11 highlights the relationship among employee involvement, total quality management, and reengineering. It shows how the outcomes of reengineering are influenced by the way in which the program is managed. The results are somewhat mixed for the three different types of reengineering outcomes, but the overall

Table 19.11 **Relationship of Reengineering Outcomes to How It Is Managed.**

	Reengineering Outcomes			
	Direct Performance Outcomes✪	Profitability and Competitiveness	Employee Satisfaction and QWL	Satisfaction with Reengineering Overall
A Separate Program	3.84	3.85	2.86	3.40
Integrated with Both TQM and EI	4.04	4.13	3.42	3.85
Integrated with TQM Only	3.68	3.64	3.08	3.67
Integrated with EI Only	3.70	4.06	3.06	3.79

✪ (Productivity, customer satisfaction, quality, and speed)
Note: Means are reported (scale of 1–5).

trend is clear. Integrating all reengineering practices with both TQM and EI produces the best results. This seems to be particularly true with respect to employee satisfaction, quality of work life, and the direct performance outcomes. The relationship with profitability and competitiveness is weaker, but here, too, the highest results come when reengineering is integrated with both TQM and EI. The worst results are obtained when reengineering is managed as a separate program.

In summary, the evidence presented in this section substantiates the close interrelationship and complementary nature of employee involvement, total quality management, and reengineering. Companies with more extensive forms of employee involvement also have a broader application of TQM practices and report higher TQM outcomes than companies with less employee involvement. The impact of TQM practices goes down when the effect of EI is eliminated and vice versa. Both EI and TQM show the most positive results when they are used in conjunction with reengineering practices. Reengineering shows the most positive outcomes when it is combined with TQM and EI. Finally, the highest impact of reengineering is achieved when EI, TQM, and reengineering are managed as an integrated program.

Employment Contract and Change Strategy

Employee involvement, total quality management, and reengineering efforts take place in the context of a larger organizational reality. Two elements of that larger organizational reality, the employment contract and the overall change strategy, are potentially related to the success of these change efforts. Although there are some speculations in the literature on organizational change about what features of an employment contract and a change strategy are likely to lead to success with EI, TQM, and reengineering change efforts, there are few firm predictions in this area and virtually no research data establishing these relationships. In the analyses that follow we will look generally at the relationships first between the employment contract and the outcomes of the three programs, and then at the relationship between characteristics of the change strategy and outcomes of the three programs.

Employment Contract. Table 20.1 shows the relationship between fourteen items concerning the employment contract and four measures of the impact of employee involvement programs. There are a number of statistically significant relationships between the features of the employment contract and the organization's overall experience with EI efforts, as well as with the direct performance, profitability, and competitiveness outcomes. However, there are surprisingly few statistical relationships with the employee satisfaction and quality-of-work-life measures.

The two contract items concerning continued employment show quite strong relationships. Continued employment based on performance and based on developing skills and knowledge are both associated with the success of EI efforts.

Answers to questions having to do with a traditional loyalty-based employment relationship (tying rewards to seniority, rewarding loyalty, and having a job for life) tend to show little relationship with the success of employee involvement efforts. This finding once again makes the point that successful employee involvement activities do not necessarily require a corporate commitment to long-term or lifetime employment.

Interestingly, rewards tied to individual performance do not show a significant relationship to EI outcomes, but when they are tied to group and organizational performance, they do, as would be expected from the EI literature, which stresses collective rewards.

Table 20.1 **Relationship of Employment Contract to Employee Involvement Outcomes (Correlation Coefficients).**

Employment Contract: Corporation Operates by	Employee Involvement Outcomes			
	Direct Performance Outcomes✪	Profitability and Competitiveness	Employee Satisfaction and QWL	Experience with Employee Involvement
Continued Employment of Individuals Based on Performance.	.27***	.22**	.02	.09
Continued Employment of Individuals Based on Continual Development of Their Skills and Knowledge.	.46***	.29***	.15*	.34***
No One Has a Secure Job.	.03	.09	−.12	−.08
Outstanding Performers Have Job for Life.	.07	.02	.11	.22***
Rewards Tied to Individual Performance.	.11	.11	.01	.10
Rewards Are Tied to Group and/or Organization Performance.	.22**	.25***	.06	.32***
Loyalty to Company Rewarded.	.13	.01	.11	.11
Rewards Tied to Seniority.	−.05	−.04	.05	−.03
Career Development Responsibility of Individual.	.00	.06	−.05	−.07
Employees Expected to Manage Own Performance with Minimum of Supervision.	.22**	.19*	.04	.10
Fits Corporate Business Strategy.	.30***	.31***	.06	.20**
Understood by Most Employees.	.21*	.16	.16*	.11
Employees Satisfied with It.	.21*	.26***	.09	.06
We Are Changing Direction So Fast, It Is Not Clear What the Contract Is.	−.05	−.08	−.12	−.17*

✪ (Productivity, customer satisfaction, quality, and speed)
Key: * = weak relationship ($p \leq .05$)
     ** = moderate relationship ($p \leq .01$)
    *** = strong relationship ($p \leq .001$)

Having an employment contract that fits the business strategy and self-management are also strongly related to the effectiveness of the employee involvement effort. These results fit with the view that EI works when individuals have information about the business, the power to influence it, and rewards that are based on its success.

Table 20.2 presents the results for total quality management, which are generally similar to the results for EI. Positive relationships appear with employment contracts that emphasize performance and the development of skills and knowledge. Having employment contracts that fit the business strategy and satisfy employees also is a positive.

Two items have a negative relationship with satisfaction and quality of work life: no one has a secure job, and it is not clear what the contract is. These two items are also negatively related to organizations having a positive experience with their TQM programs. Apparently, at least with respect to total quality management efforts, the lack of a clear employment contract and job security is a significant negative. This finding, of course, fits with the literature on TQM that emphasizes not blaming individuals and making them feel secure.

Table 20.3 looks at the relationship between the employment contract and reengineering outcomes. The results here are weaker than those obtained for employee involvement and total quality management. Basically, there is little relationship between the success of reengineering and the nature of the employment contract. The relationships that do exist are relatively similar to those for EI and TQM. For example, tying rewards to group and/or organizational performance is significantly related and is also related to the success of EI programs. These data generally support the point that reengineering programs are different from TQM and EI efforts. Through much of our research study, employee involvement and total quality management efforts seem to behave similarly while reengineering behaves differently. Perhaps this is because reengineering is based so much on structural and technical change and is less involved in trying to establish a new, more positive relationship between individuals and their work.

Overall, the evidence clearly shows that certain types of employment contracts favor change efforts like those driven by employee involvement and total quality management, specifically those contracts that emphasize performance, skills, and business strategy. Tying rewards to collective performance is one practice that also often has a positive impact.

Employment Contract: Corporation Operates by	Total Quality Management Outcomes			
	Direct Performance Outcomes❂	Profitability and Competitiveness	Employee Satisfaction and QWL	Experience with TQM
Continued Employment of Individuals Based on Performance.	.23*	.24*	.04	.10
Continued Employment of Individuals Based on Continual Development of Their Skills and Knowledge.	.24*	.38***	.02	.16
No One Has a Secure Job.	−.02	−.05	−.27**	−.31***
Outstanding Performers Have Job for Life.	−.00	−.11	.27**	.23**
Rewards Tied to Individual Performance.	.11	.21*	.18	.08
Rewards Are Tied to Group and/or Organization Performance.	.02	.05	.02	.03
Loyalty to Company Rewarded.	.12	.07	.17	.16
Rewards Tied to Seniority.	−.10	−.08	.04	.05
Career Development Responsibility of Individual.	.19	.09	−.08	−.05
Employees Expected to Manage Own Performance with Minimum of Supervision.	.10	.08	−.15	−.03
Fits Corporate Business Strategy.	.33***	.27**	.10	.16
Understood by Most Employees.	.26**	.17	.07	.09
Employees Satisfied with It.	.20*	.21*	.05	.08
We Are Changing Direction So Fast, It Is Not Clear What the Contract Is.	−.22*	−.16	−.24*	−.18*

❂ (Productivity, customer satisfaction, quality, and speed)
Key: * = weak relationship (p ≤ .05)
　　 ** = moderate relationship (p ≤ .01)
　　 *** = strong relationship (p ≤ .001)

Table 20.3

Relationship of Employment Contract to Reengineering Outcomes (Correlation Coefficients).

	Reengineering Outcomes			
Employment Contract: Corporation Operates by	Direct Performance Outcomes✪	Profitability and Competitiveness	Employee Satisfaction and QWL	Experience with Reengineering
Continued Employment of Individuals Based on Performance.	.18*	.17*	−.01	.07
Continued Employment of Individuals Based on Continual Development of Their Skills and Knowledge.	.21*	.10	.11	.14
No One Has a Secure Job.	.23**	.05	−.07	.05
Outstanding Performers Have Job for Life.	.04	.10	.08	.07
Rewards Tied to Individual Performance.	.08	.07	−.04	−.09
Rewards Are Tied to Group and/or Organization Performance.	.19*	.16*	.18*	.19*
Loyalty to Company Rewarded.	−.03	−.06	.18*	.04
Rewards Tied to Seniority.	−.05	−.03	.01	.01
Career Development Responsibility of Individual.	.11	.02	−.06	−.11
Employees Expected to Manage Own Performance with Minimum of Supervision.	−.03	−.03	−.02	.03
Fits Corporate Business Strategy.	.15	.17*	.09	.11
Understood by Most Employees.	.13	.17*	.02	.04
Employees Satisfied with It.	.14	.11	.18*	.03
We Are Changing Direction So Fast, It Is Not Clear What the Contract Is.	−.10	−.11	−.10	−.03

✪ (Productivity, customer satisfaction, quality, and speed)
Key: * = weak relationship (p ≤ .05)
  ** = moderate relationship (p ≤ .01)
  *** = strong relationship (p ≤ .001)

Change Strategy. Table 20.4 shows the relationship between measures of change strategy and the outcomes of employee involvement efforts. As was true with the employment contract, the employee satisfaction and quality-of-work-life outcome is only weakly related to the improvement strategy items. Much more strongly related are the other outcomes, one or more of which are related to seven of the strategy items.

All of the items that are positively related to the performance outcomes can be characterized as direction or consistency items. They indicate that change efforts that are tied to a business strategy, based on clear beliefs, have mission and values statements, are integrated, are long term, and are led by top management tend to have the most successful EI programs. The importance of theme, vision, and mission is further established by the negative correlation with the item asking about unrelated initiatives.

Interestingly, the item that asks about a bottom-up strategy shows no significant relationship to any outcomes. This is in marked contrast to the item that asks about top management leadership. At least with respect to employee involvement, the evidence seems to show clearly that programs are most successful when they are led by the top, not when they are a bottom-up operation. Apparently the process used to instill employee involvement does not have to be one that is based on employee involvement. Instead, it needs to be one that has a sense of vision, direction, and relationship to business strategy.

Table 20.5 shows the results for total quality management, which are quite similar to those for employee involvement. The strongest relationships, again, are with the items concerning direction. TQM programs are seen to be successful when they have a clear sense of direction that is integrated company-wide and is generally tied to the business strategy. There is also a significant relationship between two of the outcome measures and the item asking about having a three-year or more plan.

Table 20.6 presents the results for reengineering, which are quite similar to the results for employee involvement and total quality management. For example, reengineering is more successful when it has a sense of consistent direction and top management leadership. This is highlighted by the negative relationship between the outcomes and the item regarding unrelated initiatives. The results here also generally fail to show a significant relationship with satisfaction and quality of work life. The exception is an interesting one: the fact that bottom-up implementation is significantly related

Table 20.4

Relationship of Change Strategy to Employee Involvement Outcomes (Correlation Coefficients).

Performance Improvement Approach	Employee Involvement Outcomes			
	Direct Performance Outcomes✪	Profitability and Competitiveness	Employee Satisfaction and QWL	Experience with Employee Involvement
Guided by a Clearly Stated Business Strategy	.24**	.26***	.08	.35***
Guided by Clearly Stated Beliefs about What Makes an Organization Effective	.21**	.24**	.12	.38***
Guided by Mission and Values Statements	.23**	.29***	.17*	.34***
Driven by a Threat to the Organization's Survival	–.01	–.01	–.04	–.01
Made Up of a Series of Unrelated Initiatives	–.07	–.07	–.06	–.23***
Integrated Company-Wide	.12	.24**	.12	.30***
Occurring Differently in Different Business Units	.08	.05	–.14	–.01
Based on Bottom-Up Implementation Strategy	–.04	.02	–.08	.09
Same No Matter What Country Employees Work In	.07	.03	–.03	.03
Led by Top Management	.16*	.19*	.11	.28***
Based on Three-Year or More Plan	.12	.14	.12	.24***

✪ (Productivity, customer satisfaction, quality, and speed)
Key: * = weak relationship (p ≤ .05)
    ** = moderate relationship (p ≤ .01)
    *** = strong relationship (p ≤ .001)

to satisfaction and quality of life. This suggests that getting individuals involved helps reengineering to have a positive impact on employees.

Overall, unlike the situation with the employment contract, reengineering, total quality management, and employee involvement all show significant relationships to change strategies. As a general

Table 20.5

Relationship of Change Strategy to Total Quality Management Outcomes (Correlation Coefficients).

Performance Improvement Approach	Total Quality Management Outcomes			
	Direct Performance Outcomes✪	Profitability and Competitiveness	Employee Satisfaction and QWL	Experience with Employee TQM
Guided by a Clearly Stated Business Strategy	.31***	.35***	.18	.11
Guided by Clearly Stated Beliefs About What Makes an Organization Effective	.26**	.29**	.27**	.25**
Guided by a Mission and Values Statement	.32***	.25**	.25**	.27**
Driven by a Threat to the Organization's Survival	.05	−.05	.17	.05
Made Up of a Series of Unrelated Initiatives	−.16	−.15	−.18	−.13
Integrated Company-Wide	.27**	.28**	.08	.22*
Occurring Differently in Different Business Units	−.11	−.04	−.15	−.05
Based on a Bottom-Up Implementation Strategy	.02	.07	−.03	.06
Same No Matter What Country Employees Work In	.17	.11	.19	.15
Led by Top Management	.17	.14	.11	.21*
Based on a Three-Year of More Plan	.19	.20*	.18	.25**

✪ (Productivity, customer satisfaction, quality, and speed)
Key: * = weak relationship (p ≤ .05)
      ** = moderate relationship (p ≤ .01)
      *** = strong relationship (p ≤ .001)

rule, EI, TQM, and reengineering programs produce the best results when change efforts have a clear sense of direction, are integrated, and are led by top management.

The results for change strategy and the employment contract show some important patterns. Both are clearly related to the effectiveness of employee involvement, total quality management, and in the

Table 20.6	Relationship of Change Strategy to Reengineering Outcomes (Correlation Coefficients).			

| | Reengineering Outcomes | | | |
Performance Improvement Approach	Direct Performance Outcomes✪	Profitability and Competitiveness	Employee Satisfaction and QWL	Experience with Reengineering
Guided by a Clearly Stated Business Strategy	.28***	.33***	.01	.30***
Guided by Clearly Stated Beliefs About What Makes an Organization Effective	.26**	.35***	.13	.30***
Guided by Mission and Values Statements	.21*	.17*	.13	.23**
Driven by a Threat to the Organization's Survival	.07	.12	−.07	.13
Made Up of a Series of Unrelated Initiatives	−.19*	−.30***	−.03	−.20**
Integrated Company Wide	.24**	.27***	.09	.24***
Occurring Differently in Different Business Units	.03	−.06	−.06	−.02
Based on a Bottom-Up Implementation Strategy	.17*	.10	.20*	.29***
Same No Matter What Country Employees Work In	.00	−.03	−.11	.05
Led by Top Management	.35***	.33***	.08	.22**
Based on Three-Year or More Plan	.13	.15	−.02	.16*

✪ (Productivity, customer satisfaction, quality, and speed)
Key: * = weak relationship (p ≤ .05)
    ** = moderate relationship (p ≤ .01)
    *** = strong relationship (p ≤ .001)

case of change strategy, reengineering. The nature of the employment contract seems to be particularly strongly related to successful employee involvement and total quality management programs. Organizations considering these programs should make an effort to establish an employment contract that is based on performance, skill acquisition, and rewards that are tied to organizational performance.

With respect to change strategy, the results shown here for EI, TQM, and reengineering may well fit virtually any large-scale change effort in an organization. It is quite likely that most large-scale change efforts will work best when there is a clear vision and guidance provided by the company, a good fit with business strategy, and leadership from the top of the organization.

Financial Effects

What is the effect of employee involvement, total quality management, and reengineering practices on the financial performance of companies that adopt them? The answer to this question is of critical importance for the future of these three change efforts. Ultimately, in order to survive, they must show that they improve corporate performance. Currently, the available research does not provide a definitive answer.

Studies looking at a wide range of organizational and management practices are rare. Moreover, most studies do not address the question of whether the performance effects are strong enough to influence company financial performance.

There is a large body of research on the performance effects of EI and to a lesser extent of TQM and reengineering. A number of studies have examined the effects of specific EI and TQM practices on work groups, plants, offices, and production lines (see, for example, Cotton and others, 1988; Golembiewski and Sun, 1990; Ichniowski and others, 1996). In general, these studies report some positive effects and few negative effects. The results, which are important and encouraging, are consistent with the positive ratings that we have reported in earlier sections, though the results of these studies are not quite so positive.

Some studies have examined the effects of EI and related practices on performance within specific industries, such as the steel, auto, and apparel industries. For example, MacDuffie and Krafcik (1992) found that an index of ten involvement-oriented practices predicted productivity and quality in a study of auto assembly plants worldwide. These studies use many different measures of involvement, often making it difficult to know how well the findings apply to different combinations of EI practices. The focus on single industries is an advantage in that it automatically controls for many industry-specific differences in financial performance, technology, and a host of other factors that otherwise make it difficult to establish a direct relationship between management practices and financial performance. At the same time, findings from studies in one industry may not be generalizable to other industries.

Four studies have examined the effects of organizational culture on performance at the firm level. Denison (1990) looked at thirty-four firms that had done employee attitude surveys in at least part of their organization. He found that firms with culture scores showing more participation had a higher return on investment and return on sales over a period of five years after the survey. Similarly, Hansen and Wernerfelt (1989) found that a participative culture, as measured by employee surveys, was related to return on assets in sixty firms. Kotter and Heskett (1992) found a relationship between company cultures and company financial performance. Their measures of culture overlap somewhat with the practices that are part of EI and TQM. Finally, Collins and Porras (1994) compared eighteen visionary companies to their competitors and found that the visionary companies created many times more shareholder value. These studies used employee attitudes as measures of culture, but they did not measure the use of EI and TQM practices.

Several studies have shown a link between human resources management practices and firm performance. Huselid (1995) used a broad index of human resources practices that overlaps in part with our measures of EI and TQM practices. He found a significant relationship between these practices and return on assets. Huselid and Becker (1996) showed a relationship between these same human resource management practices and the market value of corporations.

We should not underestimate the difficulty of demonstrating a relationship between management practices and firm performance. Our studies show that the typical company uses most EI, TQM, and reengineering practices with only a small percentage of its workforce, and there are virtually no firms that use them on an organization-wide basis. Thus it is impossible to compare truly high users with low or nonusers in order to see how much effect these practices have when they are universally adopted. This means that the impacts must be strong in order for them to be detected in statistical analyses because there is limited variability in the degree to which firms use these approaches. In addition, since many EI, TQM, and reengineering efforts may be only a few years old, firms may still be learning how best to implement and manage them. Further, their effects may only be starting to appear in the firms' financial results because it takes time for management practices to change behaviors and for behavioral changes to result in changes in financial results.

Unfortunately, at this point, there are no data that indicate what the actual lag time is between installing management practices and changes in company performance. It seems almost certain that this lag time varies from one practice to another. For example, cost-cutting practices such as those associated with reengineering programs may have a more rapid impact than the creation of teams. In any case, lack of knowledge about lag times makes it hard to find strong relationships. Finally, how a firm is organized and managed is just one of many influences on its financial performance; thus, the relationship of this factor to performance at any point in time may be relatively weak.

In order to examine the effects of EI, TQM, and reengineering practices on firm financial performance measures, we obtained data on company performance for 1992 through 1996 from Compustat, a database that includes thousands of companies. We were able to obtain data on 892 Fortune 1000 companies for the analyses that we report. This figure is less than the total number of companies in the Fortune 1000 for several reasons. Firms that were acquired or merged before the performance data were published were not included in the database. Also, it does not provide complete coverage of the Fortune 1000 firms; it covers most firms but does not necessarily provide data on all the measures we needed for our analyses. Finally, we also drew on the industry identification data and the data on company employment levels that are reported in *Fortune*.

We used one measure of firm economic productivity: sales per employee, a simple but relatively common productivity indicator. We used five measures of financial return: return on sales, return on assets, return on investment, return on equity, and total return to investors. Some consider return on sales and return on assets to be most closely related to corporate efficiency, while return on investment, return on equity, and total return to investors are indicators of overall corporate effectiveness.

For each of our performance measures we calculated a 1993 and a 1996 result. To get the 1993 result, we averaged the 1992, 1993, and 1994 results. To get the 1996 result, we averaged the 1995 and 1996 results (1997 was not yet available when we did these analyses). We used averages because of the instability of financial performance results; numerous accounting decisions as well as environmental events can change the results for a given year in ways that may not reflect the actual performance of the companies. Averaging results across years is one way to reduce the effect of unusual conditions.

Our analysis is unique among the available studies of firm performance. The predictors are our indices of EI, TQM, and reengineering practices. Thus, we are studying the use of specific practices, not employee attitudes that may be caused by financial performance. We are studying a variety of management practices, not just those associated with EI or TQM. As a result, we can compare the effectiveness of different management approaches. We use a number of different company performance measures as outcomes, not just one or two measures. Finally, we look at the relationship of practices and performance over a multiple-year span of time.

Our statistical analyses used a number of control variables. There are strong industry effects for return measures and firm productivity. For example, sales per employee and return on investment tend to be systematically different for the steel and banking industries. Thus, we controlled for industry in our analyses. We also used performance data for all available firms, not just those that completed surveys in 1993 and 1996. We constructed a control variable for firms that did not provide a survey so that we could use their performance data for comparison purposes. We also controlled for capital intensity—that is, property, plant, and equipment per employee. It can vary systematically both across and also within industries and can greatly influence performance on financial outcome measures. Finally, we controlled for level of union membership.

We conducted separate multiple regression analyses of the effects of EI, TQM, and reengineering on each performance outcome. We first trimmed the sample by eliminating the top and bottom 1 to 1.5 percent of firms on each measure. This is a common procedure in the analysis of firm performance; it recognizes that extremely good or extremely poor performance is more likely due to temporary market conditions or other factors than to management practices. We next entered all the control variables in a block. Finally, we entered the EI indices, the TQM indices, or the reengineering indices in a block.

The control variables were strongly related to the measures of performance. They accounted for a large portion of the variance in performance, confirming the importance of controlling for them when analyses are done to determine the effects of management practices on firm performance.

The regression results reported in Table 21.1 show the relationship between EI use and performance in 1993 and 1996. The results indicate that the overall use of EI practices is significantly related to five measures of corporate performance. The strength and consistency of the relationship varies. Sales per employee is strongly related to the

Table 21.1	Regression Results for Financial Performance and EI Usage.		

		EI Use	
Financial Measure		1993	1996
Sales per Employee		***	***
Return on Sales		***	
Return on Assets		**	***
Return on Investment			***
Return on Equity		***	
Total Return to Investors			

Key: * = weak relationship (p ≤ .05)
   ** = moderate relationship (p ≤ .01)
   *** = strong relationship (p ≤ .001)

use of EI practices in both 1993 and 1996. The same pattern exists for return on assets. The results for return on sales, return on investment, and return on equity show a mixed pattern, significant in one year but not significant in the other. Total return to investors is the one measure that is not significantly related to EI usage in either 1993 or 1996, but the results are in the direction of high EI use being associated with a higher total return.

Table 21.2 presents the results for the relationship between financial results and TQM usage. There are no significant relationships for 1993 data, but there are three statistically significant relationships for 1996. Return on sales, return on assets, and return on equity all show statistically significant relationships between the use of TQM and the financial performance of the companies. There is no obvious explanation for why the 1993 results are insignificant while the 1996 results are significant.

Comparing these results to the employee involvement results reveals two interesting trends. Neither shows a significant relationship to total return to investors. Both show significant results for return on sales, return on assets, and return on equity. Sales per employee shows a strong relationship to employee involvement practices but not to TQM. Sales per employee, generally speaking, is a measure of productivity, and in some respects it is surprising that it is related to EI but not to TQM practices.

Table 21.2	Regression Results for Financial Performance and TQM Usage.	

	TQM Use	
Financial Measure	1993	1996
Sales per Employee		
Return on Sales		*
Return on Assets		**
Return on Investment		
Return on Equity		***
Total Return to Investors		

Key: * = weak relationship (p ≤ .05)
   ** = moderate relationship (p ≤ .01)
   *** = strong relationship (p ≤ .001)

Table 21.3 presents the results for the relationship between financial performance and reengineering usage in 1996. The results only cover 1996 because no reengineering data were collected in 1993. Four financial measures show strong relationships to the use of reengineering: return on sales, return on assets, return on investment, and return on equity. These strong results clearly suggest that reengineering does have an impact on financial performance.

It is important to point out here that the two kinds of reengineering practices had somewhat different impacts on performance. The work-restructuring items were positively related to financial performance—that is, more use of them clearly led to higher financial performance. Just the opposite was true with respect to the cost reduction items. More use of them tended to be associated with poorer financial performance.

There are several obvious explanations for the negative impact of cost reduction practices. It is possible that some of the downsizing and cost reduction activities damaged the firm's ability to perform. The second explanation is that companies, when they downsize and reduce cost, take large financial write-offs that cause their publicly reported accounting data to drop significantly, and this could result in the negative relationships. Of course, any initial drop in financial performance because of the cost reduction activities may be more than offset in the future as the cost reduction activities pay off in

Table 21.3	Regression Results for Financial Performance and Reengineering Usage.		

	Reengineering Use
Financial Measure	1996
Sales per Employee	
Return on Sales	***
Return on Assets	***
Return on Investment	***
Return on Equity	***
Total Return to Investors	

Key: * = weak relationship (p ≤ .05)
** = moderate relationship (p ≤ .01)
*** = strong relationship (p ≤ .001)

better financial results. At this point, we are not able to assess the validity of this argument since it requires financial data from later years. Clearly this is an issue that needs to be examined as financial data become available for 1997 and beyond.

Overall, the results show that management practices involving EI, TQM, and reengineering are strongly related to most of the measures of financial performance. Sales per employee is the one measure that was related only to the adoption of employee involvement practices. This is the most productivity-oriented measure used; thus, it is not surprising that it has slightly different relationships to the management practices than the other measures, which are more focused on profitability. It is not entirely clear why it relates more strongly to employee involvement. It leaves us with the question, does EI drive productivity more than the other practices?

We should also note that none of the measures are significantly related to total return to investors. The same result was found in our earlier studies of the impact of management practices on financial performance (Lawler, Mohrman, and Ledford, 1995). There is an obvious explanation for this. Unlike the other financial measures, which primarily measure the organization's internal operating effectiveness, the results concerning total return to investors depend very much on stock market conditions and other external conditions and events beyond the direct control of most companies. Probably because of this, our statistical analysis showed that this measure had a higher level of variance than the other measures. Thus, it is not surprising that this measure is the least strongly related to company practices.

How large is the effect of EI and TQM on corporate performance? The percentage of the performance variance that is accounted for by EI and TQM practices is relatively small in all the analyses. However, this does not mean that an increase in usage cannot have a significant impact on performance.

One way to estimate how much a change in one measure will cause another to change is to look at the effect of a one standard deviation change. Increasing the use of EI and TQM practices by one standard deviation means covering approximately an additional 30 percent of employees. Such an increase represents at least a doubling of many companies' present EI and TQM efforts, but it is achievable. In fact, a significant number of companies are already at this level.

Our 1993 study found that an increase of one standard deviation has quite noticeable effects on the performance measures (Lawler, Mohrman, and Ledford, 1995). Such an increase in coverage is associated with increases in total factor productivity of 1.0 percent; in return on assets of 1.1 percent; in return on sales of 2.0 percent; in return on investment of 2.8 percent; and in return on equity of 3.1 percent.

Table 21.4, which is taken from our 1993 study report, compares the financial performance of high, medium, and low adopters of EI and TQM practices (Lawler, Mohrman, and Ledford, 1995). It presents the results for firms within one standard deviation of the mean (medium use), those one standard deviation or more above the mean (high use), and those one standard deviation or more below the mean (low use) in the use of EI and TQM practices. These results should capture the attention of anyone concerned with firm performance, since they suggest that companies that are above average in the adoption of EI and TQM practices perform significantly better on these key financial measures. For example, in comparison to low users, high users enjoy a 63 percent higher return on sales, a 47 percent higher return on assets, a 62 percent higher return on investment, and a 37 percent higher return on equity. (Percentages are calculated by taking the difference between high and low users and comparing it to low use performance. For example, in the case of return on sales, 10.3 minus 6.3 equals 4.0, which is 63 percent of 6.3.) These are quite large differences that represent, in the case of these firms, millions of dollars of additional profits for high users.

Table 21.5 compares the financial performance of high, medium, and low users of EI during 1996. Once again, companies one standard deviation above and below the mean are separated from medium users. The results are consistent in showing that high-use corporations perform significantly better than low-use corporations. High users show a 25 percent higher return on sales, a 34 percent higher return on assets, a 26 percent higher return on investment, and a 40 percent higher rate of return on equity. As was true for the 1993 results, these are large and very impressive differences that suggest high-use companies perform much better financially.

Table 21.5 contains one measure that was not reported in 1993: return to investors. High users had a 108 percent greater return to investors than did low users (21.5 versus 44.8). Needless to say, this is an extremely large difference, particularly given the earlier regression results that showed that return to investors is not as strongly related to EI as are the other financial measures. One difference

Table 21.4   **Financial Effects of EI and TQM Usage in 1993.**

Financial Measures (Percentages)	Low Use	Medium Use	High Use
Return on Sales	6.3	8.3	10.3
Return on Assets	4.7	5.8	6.9
Return on Investment	9.0	11.8	14.6
Return on Equity	16.6	19.7	22.8

Table 21.5   **Financial Effects of EI Usage in 1996.**

Financial Measures (Percentages)	Low Use	Medium Use	High Use
Return on Sales	8.3	10.1	10.4
Return on Assets	9.2	10.6	12.3
Return on Investment	15.2	16.3	19.1
Return on Equity	19.8	22.7	27.8
Return to Investors	21.5	27.2	44.8

between these analyses is that we used control factors in the regression analysis while we did not in the comparison between high and low users. Thus, one possible explanation for this result is that companies that are high adopters of EI are also well managed and designed and positioned in a number of ways that contribute to good performance. In other words, high users may be different from low users in several ways that contribute to financial performance. Still, even if the findings do somewhat overstate the impact of EI on financial performance and stock prices, they strongly suggest that management practices can influence stock performance.

The financial effects of TQM are shown in Table 21.6. They show a general tendency for high users to outperform low users. The largest differences are on return on equity and return to investors. The differences for TQM are generally smaller than those for EI, suggesting that EI has more influence on financial performance.

Table 21.7 shows the results for reengineering. High users outperform low users on all measures. As with EI and TQM, the differences are particularly large with respect to return on equity (50 percent higher) and return to investors (18 percent higher). Overall, the results clearly support the argument that the extensive use of reengineering practices is associated with good financial performance.

Taken together, the results from 1993 and 1996 strongly suggest that high usage of total quality management, employee involvement, and reengineering is consistently associated with high performance. Companies who are high users of EI, TQM, and reengineering tend to perform significantly better. The results are particularly strong for EI and reengineering. TQM is more weakly related, suggesting that it does not have as much impact on financial performance.

| Table 21.6 | Financial Effects of TQM Usage in 1996. |

Financial Measures (Percentages)	Low Use	Medium Use	High Use
Return on Sales	9.8	9.7	8.7
Return on Assets	10.1	10.7	10.3
Return on Investment	15.6	16.6	15.3
Return on Equity	18.3	23.5	25.3
Return to Investors	23.9	33.5	27.5

| Table 21.7 | Financial Effects of Reengineering Usage in 1996. |

Financial Measures (Percentages)	Low Use	Medium Use	High Use
Return on Sales	9.9	9.4	11.7
Return on Assets	9.1	10.6	10.2
Return on Investment	13.4	16.4	15.4
Return on Equity	19.3	20.5	29.0
Return to Investors	28.5	26.7	33.7

Any time a relationship exists, we must question whether it is a causal one. In this case, it is very important to determine whether the adoption of management practices involving EI, TQM, and reengineering causes firm performance. If it does, a strong case can be made for the widespread adoption of these practices. If it doesn't, there is little reason for companies to adopt them.

There are a variety of alternative explanations for the relationships we have reported here. For example, it is possible that firms with higher rates of return adopt EI, TQM, and reengineering practices because they can afford to do so.

Our study cannot prove causality because it is correlational rather than experimental. But there is one way to rule out some alternative explanations for the relationship between EI, TQM, and reengineering practices and financial performance. Through the analysis of changes in practices and performance over time, we can reach some conclusion about causation. Because of shifts in the makeup of our sample and the changing composition of the Fortune 1000, our sample of repeated firms is too small to enable us to do an adequate longitudinal matched-sample analysis from 1987 to 1996. We can, however, examine the time-lagged relationships between employee involvement and financial performance in 1993 and 1996.

Particularly revealing with respect to causality is the comparison of the time-lagged effects of EI, TQM, and reengineering usage on financial performance to the time-lagged effects of financial performance on EI, TQM, and reengineering usage. The interpretation of these relationships is relatively straightforward. If the stronger relationships occur when practices are used to predict later financial performance, then the causal relationship is from the practice to financial performance, not the reverse. This conclusion is based on the assumption that the financial performance effects of the implementation of EI and TQM will not be observable for several years, which seems likely because of the time it takes people to learn how to perform effectively in these new ways and to introduce improvements in processes and methods.

In order to determine for our sample of companies the most likely direction of causality, we did time-lagged analyses from the 1993 practice data to the 1996 financial performance data and time-lagged analyses from the 1993 financial data to the 1996 practice data. The strongest relationships were clearly those for the 1993 practice data to the 1996 financial performance data. This provides relatively strong evidence that practices cause financial performance rather than the reverse. We should note here, however, that the lagged results were not as strong as the results reported earlier relating the 1993 and 1996 practice data to the financial performance data for the same years. This suggests that the time lag used (three years) might be too long and that the financial impact of these practices shows up more quickly. In any case, the evidence strongly argues for the interpretation that practices cause financial performance rather than the reverse.

Overall, we believe the relationship among employee involvement, total quality management, and firm performance is intriguing and significant. It strongly suggests that firms can improve their financial performance by adopting an appropriate mix of EI, TQM, and reengineering practices. Our analyses of the financial impact of these practices support the favorable ratings we received when firms were asked to evaluate the success of their EI, TQM, and reengineering programs and practices. Overall, our study suggests that EI, TQM, and reengineering work and that by adopting them on a widespread basis firms can gain a significant competitive advantage.

PART FIVE

Who Adopts Employee Involvement, Total Quality Management, and Reengineering?

Organizational Size, Downsizing, and Delayering

There are a number of reasons to believe that the adoption of EI, TQM, and reengineering may be related to the size and structure of organizations. Studies of organizations have found organizational size to be associated with the adoption of a variety of management practices. Large size in particular seems to be associated with the existence in firms of formal programs and change efforts. Downsizing and delayering are both possible results of installing EI, TQM, and reengineering. They also maybe actions that may create the need for EI, TQM, and reengineering efforts.

Organizational Size. Our previous surveys indicated that larger firms are significantly more likely than smaller ones to adopt EI and TQM practices. This was not surprising. Other researchers have found organizational size, as measured by number of employees, to be one of the best predictors of innovation adoption in general (Rogers, 1983). Larger firms tend to have greater resources for innovation, including corporate staff groups that may champion change and provide change-oriented support. They may also have a greater need for formal programs to improve their performance, since they tend to have formalized practices and procedures that make change difficult. In addition, larger organizations are more complex and diverse, which can increase the number of places where innovation can be initiated.

Larger firms are in many respects prime candidates for EI, TQM, and reengineering efforts. They often experience motivational problems because it is hard for employees and managers to see the impact of their work on the customer and on company performance. Large size can also lead to employees feeling part of an impersonal, bureaucratic system. Moreover, the work in large firms is more likely to be highly segmented, with many different groups being involved in complex processes and with many places where work-process problems can result from handoffs and conflicting priorities. Employees in large firms are therefore prime targets for the kinds of process-improvement changes that are part of TQM and reengineering programs.

Several factors work against the successful establishment and dissemination of innovation in large organizations. First, segmentation, bureaucratic structures, and the resulting rigidity can all interfere with an organization's ability to develop an effective approach to change and to disseminate successful innovations throughout. In addition, size makes it hard for large-scale change initiatives to have a quick impact on company performance. Managers may become discouraged with the pace of change, and employees may have difficulty believing that the initiatives are serious or that they can make a difference. Furthermore, most large companies have a history of change initiatives that are experienced as the "flavor of the month"; championed by different parts of the organization, they are not coordinated with each other. As a result, employees may ignore or resist most change efforts.

Table 22.1 shows the relationship between organizational size and the adoption of employee involvement practices in 1987, 1990, 1993, and 1996. It indicates that larger firms have higher adoption rates than do smaller firms. In 1996, larger firms tended to make more use of employee involvement overall and of power-sharing and knowledge-development practices in particular. The relationship with EI is relatively constant over the four time periods, particularly with respect to power sharing.

Table 22.2 shows the relationships between size and the use of TQM practices for 1990, 1993, and 1996. In 1990, the use of five of the eleven TQM practices was significantly related to organizational

Table 22.1	**Relationship Between Firm Size and Adoption of EI Practices (Correlation Coefficients).**			
Employee Involvement Practices	1987	1990	1993	1996
EI Overall	.15*	.22***	.16*	.22**
Information Overall	.07	.11	.09	.04
Knowledge and Skills Overall	.09	.09	–.01	.16*
Rewards Overall	.06	.14*	.18**	.08
Power Sharing Overall	.25***	.28***	.13*	.29***

Key: * = weak relationship (p ≤ .05)
      ** = moderate relationship (p ≤ .01)
      *** = strong relationship (p ≤ .001)

Table 22.2	Relationship Between Firm Size and Adoption of TQM Practices (Correlation Coefficients).		
Total Quality Management	**1990**	**1993**	**1996**
Core Practices Overall	n/a	.07	.27**
Quality Improvement Teams	n/a	.06	.07
Quality Councils	n/a	.07	.18*
Cross-Functional Planning	n/a	.03	.22*
Customer Satisfaction Monitoring	n/a	.13	.26**
Direct Employee Exposure to Customers	.14*	−.02	.23**
Work Simplification	.13*	.05	.12
Production-Oriented Practices Overall	n/a	.09	.25**
Self-Inspection	.15*	.09	.13
Statistical Control Method Used by Front-Line Employees	n/a	−.02	.27**
Just-in-Time Deliveries	.18**	.19**	.19*
Work Cells or Manufacturing Cells	.14*	.02	.28**
Other Practices			
Cost of Quality Monitoring	.10	−.06	.26**
Collaboration with Suppliers in Quality Efforts	.07	.05	.29***
Percentage Covered by TQM	.20***	.02	.12

Key: * = weak relationship (p ≤ .05)
    ** = moderate relationship (p ≤ .01)
    *** = strong relationship (p ≤ .001)
    n/a = not asked

size. In 1993, only one practice, the use of just-in-time deliveries, was related to size. However, in 1996 the use of almost every practice is related to organization size, clearly establishing that TQM practices are more frequently used in large companies.

Table 22.3 shows that there are no statistically significant relationships between organizational size and the adoption of reengineering practices. The correlations are generally positive, but none of them is statistically significant. There is no obvious explanation for the weakness of these relationships. Nevertheless, it does establish that reengineering has a different adoption pattern than EI and TQM.

Downsizing and Delayering. During the past decade, companies took many measures to strengthen their competitive position. Downsizing and delayering are two of the most prominent. In some cases they led the change: companies cut levels and headcount and then expected the remaining organizational members to find new ways to do things with fewer people. This approach sometimes led "through

| Table 22.3 | Relationship Between Firm Size and Adoption of Reengineering Practices (Correlation Coefficients). |

Reengineering Practices	1996
Work Structure Overall	.10
Process Simplification	.13
Creation of Cross-Functional Units	.14
Major Information System	.11
Enriched Multiskilled Individual Jobs	.02
Multiskilled Teams	−.03
Cost Reduction Overall	.10
Doing Same Work with Fewer People	.13
Doing Same Work with Less Supervision	.07
Lower Overall Cost Structure	.08
Percentage of Employees Covered by Reengineering	.10

Key: * = weak relationship ($p \leq .05$)
   ** = moderate relationship ($p \leq .01$)
   *** = strong relationship ($p \leq .001$)

the back door" to changes in processes and to employees' increased involvement and empowerment. In other cases, downsizing and delayering were the result of a planned reconfiguration of work processes. Employee involvement was encouraged by moving managerial responsibilities and decision making closer to the level at which products were developed and manufactured and services delivered.

In 1996, 51 percent of the firms studied reported that they decreased in size during the past ten years (see Table 22.4), while 45 percent reported growing in size. When compared to 1993, these results show a slightly higher percentage of firms downsized (51 percent in 1996 versus 47 percent in 1993), clearly indicating that downsizing has not gone away or even decreased. Overall, these Fortune 1000 firms show a high level of change in size, but they did not necessarily become significantly smaller. Many grew. Of course, this may not have been the experience of the typical firm during this period; here the focus is on the "winners" that belong to the Fortune 1000.

As shown in Table 22.5, 78 percent of firms have eliminated at least one layer of management in the past ten years, with over 45 percent of those having reduced two or more levels. This is a slight increase from 1993, when the figure for eliminating one or more levels stood at 71 percent. Apparently, firms continue to eliminate layers of management just as they continue to downsize. Indeed, they show a greater tendency to delayer than to downsize.

The literature on organizational effectiveness has debated whether a move toward employee involvement is possible in an environment characterized by downsizing and delayering. These activities can result in greater job insecurity and perhaps less commitment as employees lose the sense that the company will provide a job for them as long as they carry our their responsibilities. In addition, downsizing may cause increased stress as a result of work overload and insecurity. At the same time, reduction in layers of management can result in more autonomy and responsibility for line employees and fewer required approvals. Delayering also can result in swifter decision making and more ownership over decisions. In fact, in many organizations it is difficult to imagine creating meaningful employee involvement unless the size and shape of the control-oriented hierarchy are changed.

Table 22.6 shows the relationship of downsizing and removing layers to the use of employee involvement practices in 1990, 1993, and 1996 (the downsizing and delayering questions were not asked in 1987). Overall, downsized organizations are not more or less likely to have adopted employee involvement.

Table 22.4   Changes in Size of Workforce in Last Ten Years.

Approximately how much has the size of your workforce changed in the last ten years?	Percentage of Companies	
	1993	1996
Decreased by More Than 50 percent	5.1	4.3
Decreased 41 to 50 percent	6.3	3.8
Decreased 31 to 40 percent	7.4	4.8
Decreased 21 to 30 percent	9.2	15.2
Decreased 10 to 20 percent	10.7	16.7
Decreased Less Than 10 percent	8.8	6.2
No Change	4.8	4.3
Increased Less Than 20 percent	10.7	17.6
Increased 21 to 40 percent	10.3	7.6
Increased 41 to 60 percent	3.7	3.3
Increased 61 to 80 percent	2.6	1.4
Increased 81 to 100 percent	3.7	2.9
Increased More Than 100 percent	16.9	11.9

Table 22.5   Number of Layers of Management Removed During Last Ten Years.

Number of Layers Removed	Percentage of Companies	
	1993	1996
None	28.9	21.7
One	28.6	33.3
Two	32.3	31.4
Three	6.4	10.6
Four	2.6	2.4
Five	0.8	0.5
Six or More	0.4	0.0

Table 22.6	Relationship of Downsizing and Removing Layers to Employee Involvement Indices.					

	Compared to Those That Have Not					
	Firms That Have Downsized			Firms That Have Removed Layers		
	1990	1993	1996	1990	1993	1996
EI Overall					More Use	
Information Overall					More Use	
Knowledge and Skills Overall						More Use
Rewards Overall						
Power Sharing Overall					More Use	More Use

Note: "More Use" relationships are significant (p ≤ .05).

A somewhat different pattern of EI adoption distinguishes firms that have reduced management layers from those that have not. Here we see greater use of employee involvement practices, particularly of information sharing and power sharing in 1993 and of knowledge building and power sharing in 1996. Since 1990, there has been considerable growth in the number of areas of EI adoption where delayered organizations exceed those that have not delayered. The only area where there has not been greater adoption by delayered firms is in the area of rewards. Thus, it appears that flattening an organization drives and/or accompanies the introduction of EI practices while downsizing does not. This underscores the idea that creating a highly involving organization requires a redesign of an organization's structure.

Table 22.7 shows that the use of TQM practices is not positively related to downsizing or delayering in 1996. A few relationships do exist in the 1990 and 1993 data. There is no obvious reason why these relationships are not present in the more recent data. The finding that delayering in 1993 and 1996 does not seem to be associated with a greater use of TQM is a clear difference from the pattern for the use of EI. This outcome probably reflects EI's greater emphasis on restructuring and pushing decision making down.

Much of the discussion of reengineering has centered on its close relationship to downsizing and creating lateral processes that make management layers unnecessary. Thus, we have every reason to

Table 22.7 — Relationship of Downsizing and Removing Layers to Use of TQM Practices.

	Compared to Those That Have Not					
	Firms That Have Downsized			Firms That Have Removed Layers		
TQM Practices	1990	1993	1996	1990	1993	1996
Core Practices Overall						
Production-Oriented Practices Overall						
Just-in-Time Deliveries				More Use		
Work Cells or Manufacturing Cells	More Use			More Use		
Other Practices						
Cost-of-Quality Monitoring	More Use			More Use		
Collaboration with Suppliers in Quality Efforts						
Percentage of Employees Involved		More Use			Less Use	

Note: "More Use" and "Less Use" relationships are significant (p ≤ .05).

expect that the adoption of reengineering practices will be associated with both downsizing and removing layers; indeed, in some cases these two activities are almost seen as what a reengineering effort is all about. Table 22.8 shows the relationship between various reengineering practices and the use of downsizing and removing layers. Interestingly, in the case of downsizing, there is a strong relationship between the cost reduction practices and downsizing. The work-restructuring practices, however, are not associated with downsizing. The most obvious interpretation is that companies that adopt downsizing are generally in a cost reduction mode, and as they downsize they operate with fewer people and less supervision.

The results for removing layers show that both work restructuring and cost reduction practices are related to removing layers. Often, the reengineering of an organization's processes is a precondition to successful delayering, so it is not surprising to see a relationship between work structuring and delayering. The cost reduction activities of reengineering are also closely associated with removing layers,

Table 22.8	Relationship of Downsizing and Removing Layers to Use of Reengineering Practices.	
	Compared to Those That Have Not	
	Firms That Have Downsized	Firms That Have Removed Layers
Reengineering Practices	1996	1996
Work Structure Overall		More Use
Process Simplification		
Creation of Cross-Functional Units		
Major Information System		
Enriched Multiskilled Individual Jobs		More Use
Multiskilled Teams		More Use
Cost Reduction Overall	More Use	More Use
Doing Same Work with Fewer People	More Use	More Use
Doing Same Work with Less Supervision	More Use	More Use
Lower Overall Cost Structure		More Use
Percentage of Employees Covered by Reengineering	More Use	More Use

Note: "More Use" relationships are significant ($p \leq .05$).

as might be expected, since removing layers, like downsizing, is an effective way to remove costs from the organization.

Overall, downsizing does not seem to have a relationship to the implementation of EI and TQM practices. In contrast, delayering has a positive relationship to both. It is associated with greater adoption of EI practices. The situation is quite different in the case of reengineering; its adoption is associated with both downsizing and removing layers.

Impact of Competitive Environment and Business Strategy

The increased competition that many U.S. companies face has been well documented. It has spurred corporations to find ways to make improvements in speed, cost, and quality. Some business sectors have felt the impact of this competition for several decades; thus, there is good reason to believe it may have had a significant effect on how many organizations are managed. One possible response to competitive pressures is to adopt employee involvement, total quality management, and reengineering practices in order to gain the advantages they offer. In the 1990, 1993, and 1996 surveys, we asked questions about the competitive conditions that companies confront. In this section, we investigate the relationship between competitive market conditions and the adoption of EI, TQM, and reengineering practices.

Competitive Environment. Table 23.1 presents data on the competitive market conditions that companies report that they face. In 1996, two-thirds or more of the companies reported experiencing the following market conditions to at least some extent: foreign competition, shorter product life cycles, declining markets, rapid growth, quality competition, intense cost competition, rapid change, and speed-to-market competition. Intense cost competition stands out as the most commonly experienced condition. There are two changes from 1990 to 1996; the 1996 results show more companies facing rapidly growing markets and shorter product life cycles.

Table 23.2 shows that three conditions are related to the adoption of employee involvement practices in 1993 and 1996: foreign competition, rapidly growing markets, and extreme performance pressures. The most strongly related of the three are extreme performance pressures and rapidly growing markets.

The measure of extreme performance pressure was created by combining the responses to a series of statistically related questions indicating that an organization has to perform at very high levels in order to compete effectively. The items included rapid environmental change, intense cost competition, intense speed-to-market competition, shorter product life cycles, and intense quality competition. When companies face an extremely difficult competitive environment, employee involvement seems to become an attractive strategy, probably because it promises significant improvements in organizational performance rather than just the incremental change that might come about as a result of perfecting an existing management approach. The relationship between rapidly growing

Table 23.1

Percentage of Companies Reporting Characteristics of Competitive Business Environment.

Corporation's Business Environment:		Mean[1]	Little or No Extent	Some Extent	Moderate Extent	Great Extent	Very Great Extent
Subject to Heavy Foreign Competition	1990	2.5	37	21	14	17	11
	1993	2.4	32	27	15	18	9
	1996	2.5	32	27	10	20	10
Rapidly Growing Market	1990	2.2	33	32	23	9	4
	1993	2.2	35	32	19	12	3
	1996	2.7	20	28	27	11	14
Shorter Product Life Cycles	1990	2.4	33	22	26	14	6
	1993	2.5	29	24	22	20	6
	1996	2.8	24	21	23	20	13
Declining Markets	1990	2.2	30	38	19	10	4
	1993	2.4	22	35	27	12	5
	1996	2.2	32	32	21	10	4
Intense Quality Competition	1993	3.6	3	14	27	36	21
	1996	3.4	5	11	35	34	14
Intense Speed-to-Market Competition	1993	3.4	10	13	24	33	20
	1996	3.4	9	15	24	31	22
Intense Cost Competition	1993	4.4	0	2	10	32	56
	1996	4.3	1	1	13	33	52
Rapid Change	1993	3.9	1	10	24	32	32
	1996	4.0	1	8	17	36	38

[1]Scale of 1–5.
Note: 1990 data included when available.

Table 23.2

Relationship of Market Conditions to Adoption of EI Practices (Correlation Coefficients).

EI Practices	Foreign Competition		Extreme Performance Pressures[1]		Declining Markets		Rapidly Growing Markets	
	1993	1996	1993	1996	1993	1996	1993	1996
EI Overall	.17*	.08	.26***	.17*	.00	–.08	.23***	.18*
Information Overall	.10	.04	.11	.16*	.02	–.10	.15*	.19**
Knowledge Overall	.15*	.07	.20***	.17*	.02	.03	.21***	.14*
Rewards Overall	.06	.08	.20***	.00	–.07	–.15*	.23***	.12
Power Sharing Overall	.27***	.15*	.24***	.18**	.07	.06	.11	.14*

[1]Rapid change, intense cost competition, intense speed-to-market competition, shorter product life cycles, and intense quality competition.
Key: * = weak but significant (p ≤ .05)
    ** = moderate relationship (p ≤ .01)
    *** = strong relationship (p ≤ .001)

markets and the adoption of EI practices suggests that many organizations see employee involvement as a way to help them take advantage of the opportunities that growth creates.

The amount of foreign competition is also related to the adoption of some EI practices, particularly in the 1993 results. This result follows logically from the consistent relationship between performance pressure and the adoption of employee involvement. Foreign competition is usually particularly intense. The lower relationship in 1996 may suggest that foreign competition is no longer particularly tough or that there is plenty of tough domestic competition.

Declining markets appear to make little difference in the adoption of employee involvement, perhaps because a declining market makes it difficult to justify the transition costs involved in moving to EI. Moreover, managers may not view EI as a means of making the cost reductions that are often needed in a declining market. The one exception to the no relationship conclusion is reward system practices; they are actually less likely to occur in declining markets.

Table 23.3 presents the results regarding the adoption of total quality management practices. The relationships here are similar to those for the adoption of employee involvement, with one important exception. Rapidly growing markets do not have a relationship to the adoption of TQM practices in the 1996 data. However, for-

	Foreign Competition		Extreme Performance Pressures[1]		Declining Markets		Rapidly Growing Markets	
TQM Practices	1993	1996	1993	1996	1993	1996	1993	1996
Core Practices Overall	.17*	.01	.17*	.06	.04	−.05	.08	.03
Production-Oriented Practices Overall	.30***	.35***	.25***	.32***	−.04	−.05	.15*	.13
Other Practices								
Cost-of-Quality Monitoring	.15*	.22*	.15*	.18*	−.02	.02	.15*	−.01
Collaboration with Suppliers in Quality Efforts	.17*	.11	.15*	.13	−.05	−.03	.07	.07
Percentage Covered	.25***	.29***	.10	.12	.11	.02	−.04	−.01

[1]Rapid change, intense cost competition, intense speed-to-market competition, shorter product life cycles, and intense quality competition.
Key: * = weak relationship (p ≤ .05)
  ** = moderate relationship (p ≤ .01)
  *** = strong relationship (p ≤ .001)

eign competition and extreme performance pressures are clearly related to their implementation in both 1993 and 1996. Foreign competition, in fact, is more strongly related, possibly reflecting the development of a global emphasis on quality processes that has led to various internationally recognized quality process and certification programs.

Table 23.4 shows the relationship between market conditions and the adoption of reengineering practices. Although the relationships are not as strong as they are for employee involvement and total quality management, extreme performance pressures do relate to the adoption of reengineering practices, specifically those practices involving work restructuring.

Overall the results suggest that TQM, employee involvement, and reengineering are most likely to be adopted when an organization faces tough competitive pressure. This finding supports the arguments that they are effective in improving performance and that they can often be complementary to each other. It also suggests that they are not just "nice to do" activities; they are improvement approaches adopted by companies facing difficult competitive conditions.

Table 23.4

Table 23.4 Relationship of Market Conditions to Adoption of Reengineering Practices (Correlation Coefficients).

Reengineering Practices	Foreign Competition	Extreme Performance Pressures[1]	Declining Markets	Rapidly Growing Markets
Work Restructure	.06	.22**	–.06	.13
Process Simplification	.02	.13	–.15	.08
Creation of Cross-Functional Units	.14	.18*	–.06	.03
Major Information System Redesign	–.02	.24**	.06	.16*
Enriched Multiskilled Individual Jobs	.03	.17*	–.09	.11
Multiskilled Teams	.09	.11	–.05	.08
Cost Reduction	.05	.04	–.01	–.03
Doing Same Work with Fewer People	.07	.07	.00	.02
Doing Same Work with Less Supervision	–.01	–.02	–.02	–.10
Lower Overall Cost Structure	.08	.07	–.02	.00
Percentage Covered	.03	.01	–.02	.00

[1]Rapid change, intense cost competition, intense speed-to-market competition, shorter product life cycles, and intense quality competition.
Key: * = weak relationship (p ≤ .05)
  ** = moderate relationship (p ≤ .01)
  *** = strong relationship (p ≤ .001)

Business Strategy. The literature in the area of business strategy increasingly emphasizes the importance of organizations developing distinctive approaches to their markets as well as the organizational competencies and capabilities that allow them to perform in particular ways (Prahalad and Hamel, 1990; Mohrman, Galbraith, and Lawler, 1998). Organizations can take a number of different approaches to distinguish their products and services in competitive markets. Table 23.5 lists some of the major strategies that organizations use in order to gain competitive advantage. The table shows that all of these, with the exception of being global, are seen as a part of the strategy of most companies to at least some extent. About a quarter of the sample says that being global is not an

Table 23.5

Percentage of Companies Reporting Various Characteristics of Business Strategy.

	Mean[1]	Little or No Extent	Some Extent	Moderate Extent	Great Extent	Very Great Extent
Increase Percent of Revenue from New Products and Services	3.5	5	15	23	37	20
Be a Global Company	3.1	24	14	14	21	27
Develop Strong Customer Focus	4.5	1	1	7	30	62
Increase Speed with Products Brought to Market	3.5	9	13	22	29	27
Build Knowledge and Intellectual Capital	3.4	3	16	31	35	15
Become a Low-Cost Competitor	4.0	4	9	16	30	41
Ensure High Levels of Quality	4.2	0	5	11	42	41
Respond Quickly to Changes in Market	4.1	1	3	19	43	34
Be a Technology Leader	3.7	4	11	27	28	30

[1]Mean based on a scale of 1–5.

important part of their business strategy—hardly a surprising finding in a sample that includes some companies engaged in domestic businesses that traditionally have not been global (for example, insurance and utilities).

The most popular strategy appears to be developing a strong customer focus. Again, this is hardly surprising; regardless of a company's product or service, customer focus is a highly desirable and necessary organizational capability that has received a great deal of attention in the management literature during the last decade. Other highly rated strategies include lowering costs, improving quality, and improving speed.

Implementation is a significant challenge for any strategy. It is one thing to make "being close to customers" a strategy and quite another to put in place the practices and policies that will create a customer-focused organization. Employee involvement, total quality management, and reengineering all offer practices that can contribute to the development of strategically important organizational capabilities. However, it is unlikely that EI, TQM, and reengineering are equally effective in aiding the implementation of all business strategies. Thus, a key question concerns the degree to which different strategies cause firms to use EI, TQM, and reengineering practices.

Table 23.6 reports on the relationship between business strategy and the adoption of employee involvement practices. It clearly shows that employee involvement is strongly associated with six of the nine strategies. It is particularly strongly associated with devel-

---

Table 23.6 **Relationship of Business Strategy to Adoption of EI Practices (Correlation Coefficients).**

| Business Strategy | EI Practices | | | | |
	EI Overall	Information Sharing	Knowledge and Skills Development	Rewards	Power Sharing
Increase Percentage of Revenue from New Products and Services	.09	.10	.09	.05	.08
Be a Global Company	.17*	.15*	.12	.11	.14
Develop Strong Customer Focus	.33***	.26***	.23***	.14	.31***
Increase Speed with Products Brought to Market	.25***	.28***	.25***	.05	.18**
Build Knowledge and Intellectual Capital	.32***	.28***	.31***	.05	.25***
Become a Low-Cost Competitor	–.01	.06	.04	–.06	–.03
Ensure High Levels of Quality	.23**	.18**	.29***	.05	.27***
Respond Quickly to Changes in Market	.19*	.23***	.19**	.05	.12
Be a Technology Leader	.29***	.28***	.20**	.13	.17*

Key: * = weak relationship (p ≤ .05)
** = moderate relationship (p ≤ .01)
*** = strong relationship (p ≤ .001)

---

oping a strong customer focus, speeding products to market, and building knowledge and intellectual capital. It is less but still significantly related to ensuring high levels of quality, responding quickly to change, and being a technology leader. In general, the results fit what might be expected for employee involvement. The literature on EI does not link it to being global or to reducing costs. It is surprising that it is not related to increasing the percent of revenue from new products and services, since there is evidence that product development can be facilitated by broad involvement in the product development process and that a certain amount of involvement can help encourage innovation (Mohrman, Cohen, and Mohrman, 1995).

The employee involvement practices involving rewards clearly behave differently from those involving information, knowledge, and power. The reward items are not related to the adoption of any of the strategy approaches. It is impossible to determine why this is true, but at least one possibility may be that the different business strategies impact more on what is measured in pay-for-performance plans than on the adoption of the particular kinds of pay practices that are oriented toward employee involvement.

Table 23.7 shows the relationship between business strategy and the adoption of TQM practices. The results show a pattern of significant relationships between five strategy approaches and the adoption of TQM practices. As is true with employee involvement, increasing revenue from new products and services is not among the strategies that show significant relationships. Unlike the results for employee involvement, building knowledge and responding quickly to market changes are not strongly related to the adoption of TQM practices. Also unlike the results for EI, being a global company is significantly related to adoption of TQM. This is consistent with the result found earlier concerning the competitive environment; both suggest that a focus on quality is an important part of operating a global company.

As is shown in Table 23.8, the adoption of reengineering practices is related to certain approaches to business strategy. It is significantly related to six of the nine strategy items. Specifically, it is most frequently adopted when organizations are striving to build knowledge, lower costs, improve quality, and respond quickly to the market. Work restructuring reengineering practices are associated with being a technology leader and increasing speed.

There are some interesting differences in the relationship between strategy and the adoption of the two different kinds of reengineering

Table 23.7 — Relationship of Business Strategy to Adoption of TQM Practices (Correlation Coefficients).

Business Strategy	TQM Practices				
	Percent TQM Covered	Core TQM Practices[1]	Production-Oriented Practices[2]	Cost-of-Quality Monitoring	Collaboration with Suppliers in Quality Efforts
Increase Percentage of Revenue from New Products and Services	.06	.00	.13	.17*	.05
Be a Global Company	.27***	.13	.42***	.27**	.23**
Develop Strong Customer Focus	.16*	.30***	.32***	.19*	.23**
Increase Speed with Products Brought to Market	.07	.16	.43***	.30***	.25**
Build Knowledge and Intellectual Capital	−.01	.15	.26**	.10	.20*
Become a Low-Cost Competitor	.05	.01	.06	.06	.08
Ensure High Levels of Quality	.19**	.41***	.36***	.33***	.36***
Respond Quickly to Changes in Market	−.07	.01	.12	.08	.16
Be a Technology Leader	.08	.13	.33***	.23**	.26**

[1]Quality improvement teams, quality circles, cross-functional planning, work simplification, customer satisfaction monitoring, direct exposure to customers.
[2]Self-inspection, statistical control method, just-in-time deliveries, work cells, or manufacturing cells.
Key: * = weak relationship (p ≤ .05)
** = moderate relationship (p ≤ .01)
*** = strong relationship (p ≤ .001)

practices. Cost reduction practices tend not to be associated with speed to market, while work restructuring is. This is not a surprising outcome, since cost reduction is not normally associated with increasing speed. In fact, perhaps the most surprising thing is that there is not a negative relationship here. On the other hand, work restructuring is generally thought to be significantly related to bringing products to market more quickly.

The results for being a low-cost competitor are just the reverse of those associated with speed to market. Work-restructuring practices

Table 23.8

Table 23.8 Relationship of Business Strategy to Adoption of Reengineering Practices (Correlation Coefficients).

Business Strategy	Reengineering Practices										
	Work Restructure	Process Simplification	Cross-Functional Units	Information System	Multi-skilled Individual Jobs	Multi-skilled Teams	Cost Reduction	Same Work—Fewer People	Same Work—Less Supervision	Lower Overall Cost Structure	Percentage Covered
Increase Percent of Revenue from New Products and Services	.09	−.01	.11	.11	.07	.05	.02	.01	.02	.02	−.09
Be a Global Company	.04	.02	.06	−.03	−.01	.09	.16*	.14	.13	.17*	.07
Develop Strong Customer Focus	.14	.08	.17*	.15	.06	.07	.08	.09	.08	.05	.03
Increase Speed with Products Brought to Market	.31***	.17*	.27***	.20**	.24***	.27***	.11	.13	.04	.12	.06
Build Knowledge and Intellectual Capital	.34***	.27***	.29***	.15*	.26***	.32***	.22**	.17*	.22**	.20**	.10
Become a Low-Cost Competitor	.09	.15*	.07	−.01	.07	.10	.31***	.26***	.27***	.28***	.07
Ensure High Levels of Quality	.30***	.26***	.27***	.27***	.21**	.17*	.28***	.28***	.25***	.22**	.10
Respond Quickly to Changes in Market	.31***	.20**	.23**	.27***	.16*	.23**	.21**	.20**	.13	.23**	.10
Be a Technology Leader	.23**	.17*	.19*	.14	.20**	.18*	.09	.12	.03	.08	.01

Key: * = weak relationship (p ≤ .05)
     ** = moderate relationship (p ≤ .01)
     *** = strong relationship (p ≤ .001)

are not strongly associated with being a low-cost competitor, while cost reductions are, as would be expected.

As can be seen in Table 23.9, which is a general summary of the relationship reported in Tables 23.6, 23.7, and 23.8, eight of the nine strategies are associated with the adoption of one or more of employee involvement, TQM, and reengineering. The one that is not associated with any is increasing the percent of revenue from new products and services. Apparently none of the practices associated

	Employee Involvement	TQM	Reengineering
Increase Percent of Revenue from New Products and Services			
Be a Global Company		Yes	
Develop Strong Customer Focus	Yes	Yes	
Increase Speed with Products Brought to Market	Yes	Yes	Yes
Build Knowledge and Intellectual Capital	Yes		Yes
Become a Low-Cost Competitor			Yes
Ensure High Levels of Quality	Yes	Yes	Yes
Respond Quickly to Changes in Market			Yes
Be a Technology Leader	Yes	Yes	

Table 23.9 Relationship of Business Strategy to Adoption of Practices.

with EI, TQM, or reengineering are seen as improving innovation or focusing organizations on the development of new products. Indeed, none of them—with the possible exception of EI—particularly claims to be effective in these areas.

Being global is associated only with the adoption of TQM practices. In one way, this is understandable since quality is such a pervasive issue internationally. But employee involvement, in many cases, has been shown to improve the quality performance of organizations as well. Thus, it is a bit surprising that being a global company is not more strongly associated with the adoption of EI practices. Customer focus is associated with employee involvement and TQM but not with reengineering. Again, this is hardly surprising since both EI and TQM have a long history of focusing on customers and creating and installing practices that allow for superior levels of customer service.

Increasing speed to market is associated with all three kinds of practices. One additional point needs to be highlighted here, however; it is not associated with cost reduction reengineering practices or with the core TQM practices, only with other TQM and reengineering practices.

Building knowledge and intellectual capital is strongly associated with employee involvement. There are a number of possible reasons for this but perhaps the main one is that knowledge work and knowledge workers are most often attracted to situations where they get large amounts of information, knowledge, power, and rewards. Somewhat surprising is the relationship between building knowledge and intellectual capital and reengineering practices. It is perhaps somewhat understandable why the work restructuring and reengineering practices are related, but cost reduction practices typically do not lead to building knowledge and intellectual capital.

Becoming a low-cost competitor is clearly linked to only one set of practices—the cost reduction aspects of reengineering. Ensuring quality, on the other hand, is strongly related to total quality management and to reengineering. The relationship with employee involvement is somewhat weaker.

Responding quickly to the market is clearly seen as most strongly influenced by the reengineering practices. This fits well with the emphasis in reengineering on simplifying processes and creating vertical alignments.

Finally, being a technology leader shows a relationship, although not a strong one, to all three sets of practices. It is not particularly surprising that this relationship is weak; it probably reflects the fact that none of these practices directly emphasizes technology leadership, although TQM focuses on it in a somewhat indirect way.

Perhaps the best conclusion that can be reached concerning the relationships between strategy and the practices associated with EI, TQM, and reengineering is that the relationships are understandable and largely to be expected. Different strategies do seem to be associated with the adoption of different practices. This fits well with the arguments in the organizational effectiveness literature that strategy should determine the structure and practices of an organization. Our data suggest that this is exactly what happens when companies consider adopting employee involvement, total quality management, and reengineering. They look at the kind of performance capabilities they need in order to implement their strategy, and they choose those practices that produce these capabilities.

SECTION 24

Performance Improvement and Change Strategy

Decisions about whether to adopt employee involvement, total quality management, and reengineering are not made in a vacuum. They are often part of a larger organizational change program that involves key changes in the organization's structure and strategy. This section focuses on whether there is a relationship between the kinds of practices that are adopted by corporations and their improvement and change strategies.

Table 24.1 shows the relationship among various performance improvement strategies and the adoption of employee involvement practices. It shows a consistent pattern of positive correlations between the eleven performance improvement items, and the indices of employee involvement practices. The one exception to the general pattern once again concerns the area of rewards, as the reward system practices seem to be only weakly related to the performance improvement strategies. The rest of the EI indices are all strongly related to most of the performance improvement approaches.

The items that enjoy the most consistently positive relationship involve building team-based organizations and organizing around competencies. Not surprisingly, knowledge development is strongly related to the degree to which the improvement strategy emphasizes the competencies of employees. Similarly, power-sharing practices are strongly related to the degree to which the strategy focuses on core competencies and the competencies of employees. Power sharing is also strongly related to building a team-based organization.

Table 24.2 presents the relationship between total quality management practices and the performance improvement strategy items. There are a number of relationships that are positive, and some of these are quite strong. Particularly impressive is the strong relationship between building a team-based organization and the adoption of all kinds of TQM practices. The adoption of TQM practices is also strongly associated with the use of project teams, a focus on core competencies of the organization, and outsourcing.

Table 24.3 presents the results for reengineering and the performance improvement strategy items. The results here show strong positive correlations with the measures of reengineering activity. Only two performance improvement approaches—reducing the number of different business units and creating global business units—fail to show consistently strong positive correlations with the reengineering practices. Particularly strong correlations exist between the adoption of reengineering and building a team-based

Table 24.1

Relationship of Improvement Strategies to Employee Involvement Practices (Correlation Coefficients).

Improvement Strategies	EI Overall	EI Practices			
		Information Sharing	Knowledge and Skills Development	Rewards	Power Sharing
Reduce Number of Different Businesses	.16*	.10	.11	.13	.15*
Create Global Business Units	.15*	.08	.08	.17*	.13
Reduce Size of Corporate Staff	.24***	.10	.23***	.16*	.23***
Restructure Corporation by Creating New Units and Eliminating Old Ones	.24***	.13	.19**	.12	.25***
Build Team-Based Organization	.36***	.26***	.35***	.13	.40***
Use Temporary Project Teams to Perform Core Work	.24***	.26***	.21**	.03	.23***
Focus on Core Competencies	.36***	.27***	.32***	.13	.36***
Outsource Work That Is Not One of the Core Competencies or Can Be Done More Cheaply Externally	.27***	.18**	.20**	.14	.25***
Emphasize the Competencies of Employees	.36***	.29***	.33***	.15*	.34***
Significant Adoption of New Information Technology	.21**	.13	.18**	.09	.23***
Introduce New Performance Measures	.29***	.22**	.23***	.14	.31***

Key: * = weak relationship (p ≤ .05)
     ** = moderate relationship (p ≤ .01)
    *** = strong relationship (p ≤ .001)

| | **Table 24.2** | **Relationship of Improvement Strategies to Total Quality Management Practices (Correlation Coefficients).** |

	TQM Practices				
Improvement Strategies	Percent TQM Covered	Core TQM Practices[1]	Production-Oriented Practices[2]	Cost-of-Quality Monitoring	Collaboration with Suppliers in Quality Efforts
Reduce Number of Different Businesses	.16*	.14	.10	.07	.16
Create Global Business Units	.19**	.11	.33***	.18*	.16
Reduce Size of Corporate Staff	.10	.24**	.21*	.08	.31***
Restructure Corporation by Creating New Units and Eliminating Old Ones	.01	.13	.19*	.10	.16
Build Team-Based Organization	.21**	.35***	.63***	.35***	.40***
Use Temporary Project Teams to Perform Core Work	.04	.24**	.38***	.19*	.30***
Focus on Core Competencies	.11	.32***	.47***	.27**	.36***
Outsource Work That Is Not One of the Core Competencies/Be Done More Cheaply Externally	.07	.32***	.32***	.18*	.32***
Emphasize the Competencies of Employees	.11	.29***	.26**	.13	.24**
Significant Adoption of New Information Technology	−.01	.20*	.11	.03	.10
Introduce New Performance Measures	−.02	.19*	.24**	.16	.19*

[1]Quality improvement teams, quality circles, cross-functional planning, work simplification, customer satisfaction monitoring, direct exposure to customers.
[2]Self-inspection, statistical control method, just-in-time deliveries, work cells, or manufacturing cells.
Key: * = weak relationship ($p \leq .05$)
  ** = moderate relationship ($p \leq .01$)
  *** = strong relationship ($p \leq .001$)

Table 24.3

Relationship of Improvement Strategies to Reengineering Activities (Correlation Coefficients).

Business Strategy	Reengineering Activities										
	Work Restructure	Process Simplification	Cross-Functional Units	Information System	Multi-skilled Individual Jobs	Multi-skilled Teams	Cost Reduction	Same Work—Fewer People	Same Work—Less Supervision	Lower Overall Cost Structure	Percentage Covered
Reduce Number of Different Businesses	.08	.05	.06	.14	.03	.05	.13	.09	.05	.21**	.03
Create Global Business Units	.15*	.00	.11	.16*	.11	.19*	.15	.16*	.09	.15	.10
Reduce Size of Corporate Staff	.18*	.20**	.14	.04	.13	.21**	.48***	.47***	.41***	.41***	.27***
Restructure Corporation by Creating New Units and Eliminating Old Ones	.22**	.12	.21**	.09	.20**	.26***	.29***	.29***	.23**	.27***	.17*
Build Team-Based Organization	.42***	.21**	.36***	.24***	.32***	.45***	.30***	.23**	.30***	.28***	.22***
Use Temporary Project Teams to Perform Core Work	.36***	.20**	.26***	.23**	.30***	.41***	.30***	.26***	.25***	.28***	.31***
Focus on Core Competencies	.45***	.25***	.40***	.31***	.31***	.45***	.33***	.29***	.22**	.37***	.24***
Outsource Work That Is Not One of the Core Competencies/ Be Done More Cheaply Externally	.35***	.23**	.29***	.18*	.30***	.34***	.32***	.32***	.31***	.24**	.28***
Emphasize the Competencies of Employees	.45***	.24***	.33***	.38***	.30***	.43***	.31***	.25***	.27***	.32***	.23***
Significant Adoption of New Information Technology	.47***	.26***	.30***	.57***	.30***	.30***	.20**	.15	.13	.26***	.21**
Introduce New Performance Measures	.35***	.15	.28***	.26***	.25***	.36***	.28***	.25***	.22**	.26***	.21**

Key: * = weak relationship (p ≤ .05)
  ** = moderate relationship (p ≤ .01)
  *** = strong relationship (p ≤ .001)

organization, focusing on core competencies, and emphasizing the competencies of employees.

Overall, there is a strong relationship between a company's performance improvement approach and the adoption of employee involvement, total quality management, and reengineering. This suggests that organizations do not randomly choose one of these three approaches and proceed with it. Instead, they adopt a pattern of practices that supports the development of the kind of organization that they need to become in order to be effective.

This point is particularly clear in the contrast between building a team-based organization and creating global business units. Organizations that say that building a team-based organization is their major strategy are more likely to adopt employee involvement, total quality management, and reengineering practices. On the other hand, creating global business units is strongly related to the adoption of TQM, which fits with the fact that quality is a critical global issue. Focusing on core competencies seems to lead to the adoption of a wide range of organizational practices. In many respects, this makes sense, since neither EI, TQM, or reengineering is necessarily the "best" way to develop all of the organizational capabilities that an organization may need or to give employees the competencies that they need to support particular organizational improvement efforts.

Change Strategy. Table 24.4 shows the relationships between the adoption of EI practices and different change strategies. Overall, there is a consistent positive relationship between six of the change strategy items and the employee involvement practices. They show a clear relationship to many of the same change strategy items that are related to the effectiveness of employee involvement—specifically, items concerned with clear guidance of the change process, integration on a company-wide basis, and leadership by senior management. Finally, the long-term orientation item also shows a significant positive correlation. Noticeably not related to the adoption of EI practices is the question concerning organizational survival. Apparently organizations that are changing in order to survive are not particularly likely to adopt employee involvement practices, probably because these practices do not produce fast bottom-line results.

Adoption of reward system practices do not seem to be well predicted by any of the change strategy items. Once again, this area behaves quite differently from information sharing, knowledge development, power sharing, and the overall employee involvement index.

Table 24.4

Relationship of Change Strategies to Employee Involvement Practices (Correlation Coefficients).

Change Strategies	EI Practices				
	EI Overall	Information Sharing	Knowledge and Skills Development	Rewards	Power Sharing
Guided By Clearly Stated Business Strategy	.44***	.41***	.39***	.14	.34***
Guided by Clearly Stated Beliefs About What Makes an Organization Effective	.39***	.31***	.40***	.11	.38***
Guided by Mission and Value Statements	.39***	.35***	.38***	.08	.37***
Driven by Threat to Organization's Survival	.02	.04	.04	−.03	.12
Made Up of a Series of Unrelated Initiatives	−.10	−.10	−.14*	.13	−.10
Integrated Company-Wide	.37***	.29***	.36***	.13	.35***
Occurring Differently in Different Business Units	.07	.00	.04	.01	.12
Based on a Bottom-Up Implementation Strategy	.10	.06	.06	.03	.19**
Same No Matter What Country Employees Work In	.07	.12	.09	.08	.08
Led by Top Management	.28***	.24***	.24***	.14	.26***
Based on Three-Year or More Plan	.26***	.26***	.22***	.09	.28***

Key: * = weak relationship (p ≤ .05)
   ** = moderate relationship (p ≤ .01)
   *** = strong relationship (p ≤ .001)

Table 24.5 presents the results for total quality management; they are similar to those for employee involvement. A strong relationship exists among a significant number of the change strategy items and the adoption of both core and production-oriented TQM practices. Again, the items concerned with strategy, mission, and leadership show the strongest relationships. One additional item is also related to the adoption of total quality management: that changes are the same in all countries. Apparently, in the case of total quality

| Table 24.5 | Relationship of Change Strategies to Total Quality Management Practices. |

Change Strategies	Percentage TQM Covered	Core TQM Practices[1]	Production-Oriented Practices[2]	Cost-of-Quality Monitoring	Collaboration with Suppliers in Quality Efforts
Guided by Clearly Stated Business Strategy	.08	.49***	.43***	.26**	.44***
Guided by Clearly Stated Beliefs About What Makes an Organization Effective	.10	.37***	.34***	.22*	.34***
Guided by Mission and Value Statements	.19**	.39***	.35***	.27**	.28***
Driven by Threat to Organization's Survival	.16*	.14	.06	−.02	.06
Made Up of a Series of Unrelated Initiatives	.06	−.27**	−.13	−.17	−.14
Integrated Company-Wide	.06	.43***	.35***	.24**	.41***
Occurring Differently in Different Business Units	−.01	−.09	.00	−.01	−.03
Based on a Bottom-Up Implementation Strategy	−.03	.05	.10	−.05	.08
Same No Matter What Country Employees Work In	.10	.41***	.36***	.27**	.35***
Led by Top Management	.11	.40***	.43***	.18*	.34***
Based on Three-Year or More Plan	.14*	.40***	.26**	.12	.18*

[1]Quality improvement teams, quality circles, cross-functional planning, work simplification, customer satisfaction monitoring, direct exposure to customers.
[2]Self-inspection, statistical control method, just-in-time deliveries, work cells, or manufacturing cells.
Key: * = weak relationship (p ≤ .05)
** = moderate relationship (p ≤ .01)
*** = strong relationship (p ≤ .001)

management, those change strategies that lead to high levels of adoption typically are top-down, clearly driven, and led by a strong vision and senior management. They also allow few local modifications, and they tend to be oriented toward the long term.

Table 24.6 presents the results for reengineering. These results are similar to those for TQM and employee involvement. Reengineering practices tend to be adopted when programs are driven by a clear strategy, mission, and beliefs, and where top management support and company-wide integration exist. Reengineering, like total quality management, tends to be associated with long-term plans. The use of reengineering practices is not associated with how consistent change activities are from country to country or from business unit to business unit.

To a great extent, our results suggest that reengineering and TQM programs tend to be implemented with change programs that are organization-wide, guided by a business strategy and mission, and led from the top. The same is generally true of EI programs, although the correlations are not quite as strong here. In many ways, the reengineering and TQM results are not surprising. Both these programs are typically sold as something that needs to be implemented in a consistent top-down way and led by senior management.

The literature on employee involvement talks more about bottom-up strategies and does not emphasize as much the need for organization-wide efforts. Our results, however, suggest that EI practices are not associated with bottom-up efforts but with efforts that are company-wide and led by the top.

In the kind of large organizations that we are studying, top-led change, of course, may be the only way to produce significant change in areas as complicated as employee involvement, reengineering, and total quality management. Putting the practices associated with these programs into place is a complex effort that requires changing multiple systems within an organization; it may be unrealistic to argue that they should be installed in anything other than a relatively top-led change effort. This is particularly likely to be true given the history of relatively hierarchical management in most of our sample companies. It also fits with the earlier finding that programs are more successful when their implementation takes a top-down approach. In essence, the data indicate that the most effective way to change a traditional hierarchical organization is by having the hierarchy lead the change process.

Table 24.6

Relationship of Change Strategies to Reengineering Activities (Correlation Coefficients).

Change Strategies	Reengineering Activities										
	Work Restructure	Process Simplification	Cross-Functional Units	Information System	Multi-skilled Individual Jobs	Multi-skilled Teams	Cost Reduction	Same Work—Fewer People	Same Work—Less Supervision	Lower Overall Cost Structure	Percentage Covered
Guided by Clearly Stated Business Strategy	.42***	.32***	.34***	.30***	.32***	.31***	.26***	.21**	.22**	.26***	.18**
Guided by Clearly Stated Beliefs About What Makes an Organization Effective	.41***	.24***	.32***	.33***	.27***	.38***	.25***	.21**	.26***	.21**	.18**
Guided by Mission and Value Statements	.31***	.27***	.26***	.20**	.20**	.25***	.23**	.16*	.23**	.21**	.08
Driven by Threat to Organization's Survival	.06	.09	.10	.00	−.02	.06	.17*	.12	.11	.21**	.14*
Made Up of a Series of Unrelated Initiatives	−.26***	−.23**	−.26***	−.21**	−.12	−.19*	−.20**	−.14	−.20**	−.19*	−.16*
Integrated Company-Wide	.42***	.29***	.40***	.35***	.23**	.30***	.23**	.14	.24***	.25***	.16*
Occurring Differently in Different Business Units	.02	−.04	−.05	.06	.04	.05	.07	.11	.06	.02	.07
Based on a Bottom-Up Implementation Strategy	.21**	.23**	.16*	.05	.21**	.20**	.05	.00	.03	.10	.12
Same No Matter What Country Employees Work In	.09	.07	.08	.01	.07	.11	.08	.09	.04	.08	.11
Led by Top Management	.33***	.23**	.30***	.26***	.13	.29***	.22**	.15	.17*	.28***	.15*
Based on Three-Year or More Plan	.28***	.18*	.23**	.20**	.16*	.30***	.21**	.21**	.18*	.17*	.18**

Key: * = weak relationship (p ≤ .05)
      ** = moderate relationship (p ≤ .01)
      *** = strong relationship (p ≤ .001)

Overall, even though employee involvement, total quality management, and reengineering are quite different approaches to improving organizational performance, their adoption seems to be associated with many of the same general conditions. They are particularly likely to be adopted when an organization is focusing on teams, core competencies, and the development of individual competencies. They also all tend to be associated with the same general type of change process—one that is led by senior management and is guided by a sense of overall direction, mission, and consistency. Thus, in some respects, employee involvement, total quality management, and reengineering are more similar than different. They are adopted by organizations that are looking to organizational effectiveness and senior-management-led organizational change processes as a key to improving their performance.

Conclusion

Toward High Performance Organizations

A burgeoning global economy, the revolution in information technology, rapid advances in scientific knowledge, and a host of other important changes have converged to create a very different business environment than the one that existed in 1987 when we did our first study of Fortune 1000 companies. Our subsequent studies of these companies document just how much change has occurred in the way corporations are managed. The changes we have found suggest that companies are increasingly looking to organizational practices, structures, and arrangements as a powerful and often sustainable source of competitive advantage.

The challenge in obtaining competitive advantage through a corporation's ability to organize itself is that there are many seemingly attractive approaches among which to choose but no one well-developed road map to success. Often change programs within companies include false steps, missteps, and restarts. Although these can be discouraging, they should not obscure the fundamental point that learning how to organize and how to change an organization in response to a dynamic environment is a critical—perhaps the most critical—capability that an organization can develop.

Our studies show how and why organizations are changing their management practices with respect to the adoption of employee involvement, total quality management, and reengineering. They also identify the results of these changes and can help guide corporations' change programs. This section highlights the most important findings and implications.

Employee Involvement. The results from our 1996 study clearly show that more and more companies are using EI practices as an important part of their approach to managing. The three studies we have done since the first in 1987 have all shown successively higher usage of employee involvement practices.

Looking first at the data on information sharing, the 1996 data show the highest levels ever with respect to sharing all types of financial information with employees. Nevertheless, there is still a tremendous opportunity for greater sharing of business information with employees, particularly information about business operating results, competitors' performance, business plans and goals, and new technologies.

The results regarding knowledge development also show growth in the amount of training and development that corporations are doing. The growth from 1993 to 1996 is small, however, much as it has been since we first started studying this topic in 1987. Further, there remains a considerable gap between what might be considered an optimal amount of training and development and what organizations are actually doing.

The reward system practices of companies are continuing to shift in ways that support employee involvement. This is perhaps most apparent with respect to the use of knowledge-or skill-based pay and the adoption of systems that reward collective performance and thus encourage teams and individuals to be involved in the business units of which they are a part. The growth in reward system practices supportive of EI is, however, relatively small. It leaves a tremendous gap between what an ideal profile might look like with respect to the adoption of practices like gainsharing, profit sharing, and employee stock ownership, and what is actually occurring.

The biggest changes are in the area of power sharing. Particularly noticeable is the growth in employee participation groups other than quality circles and in survey feedback processes. Perhaps more significant from the point of view of creating a high performance organization, however, is the growth in self-managing work teams and minibusiness units. These, along with job enrichment, have grown faster than any other practice, and they represent decisive moves toward giving individuals more responsibility for the management of the businesses of which they are a part. We must point out, however, that despite the rapid growth in these practices, they still affect only a small percentage of the total workforce in organizations.

Responses to a question asked for the first time in 1993 confirm the fact that a small minority of employees in the Fortune 1000 companies work in a high involvement situation. This question, which asked companies to describe the patterns of involvement practices covering their workers, showed that in 1993 only about 10 percent of the workforce had sufficient amounts of information, knowledge, power, and rewards to be involved in the business matters of their company. The results for 1996 show a small increase to 12 percent. Obviously, there remains an enormous gap between the potential number of employees who could be in a high involvement work setting and those who actually are.

Overall, the 1996 results on employee involvement suggest a continuation of the pattern that we have seen since 1987: a growing use of many EI practices, leading to small pockets of employee involvement in a number of companies, but few if any companies with an organization-wide high involvement approach to management. This trend may reflect either a decision by organizations that there are only certain areas in their companies where an employee involvement approach is appropriate or a decision to try employee involvement in certain areas in order to learn about it before spreading it to the entire organization.

Our analysis of who adopts EI practices strongly suggests that they are adopted by organizations who see EI as a useful competitive strategy. This conclusion is reinforced by the finding that companies that face extreme performance pressure and foreign competition are particularly likely to adopt employee involvement. There is also a relationship between the overall business improvement strategies of companies and their adoption of EI practices. For example, organizations that are focusing on their core competencies and emphasizing the competencies of employees are likely to adopt employee involvement. In addition, organizations that have clear, unified change strategies are particularly likely to adopt EI practices.

Overall, our results suggest that employee involvement is frequently part of a reasonably complete and well thought out change strategy for an organization. They also suggest that the adoption of employee involvement is usually associated with a business imperative. This argues that there will be a continued growth in the use of EI practices. They clearly are not just a fad but are practices that address important business issues. As long as they are believed to be effective, their use is likely to continue to grow.

Total Quality Management. We first studied total quality management in 1990. When we studied it again in 1993, we saw a small amount of growth in its popularity. Our 1996 data suggest that this trend has not continued. Indeed, comparing the 1990 and 1996 results suggests a stable number of companies who have TQM programs. What is growing is the use of certain TQM practices. Among the increasingly popular ones are work simplification, direct exposure to customers, work cells, self-inspection, and collaboration with suppliers. This trend may suggest that while overall TQM programs may never be accepted on a widespread basis, some of TQM's key practices will be.

As was true with employee involvement, corporations seem to adopt total quality management practices to match particular business strategies and needs. Foreign competition and extreme performance pressures are particularly strongly related to the adoption of certain TQM practices. Also related are key emphases such as being a global company, focusing on customers, and, not surprisingly, emphasizing quality for competitive advantage. TQM practices tend to be adopted when organizations have definite, well-developed change strategies. They are also most frequently adopted when an organization is focusing on core competencies and the competencies of its employees.

We may be heading into an era in which a constant number of companies are committed to total quality management programs but where a growing number find some of the TQM practices to be a useful part of their overall approach to organizing. Certain practices from TQM appear to be on the road to being widely accepted simply as conventional wisdom and good management rather than as part of a specific total quality management program. In this respect, TQM may be rated as highly successful, even though as a program its adoption is not growing and perhaps is even decreasing. Since organizations seem to adopt TQM programs for strategic purposes, there is good reason to believe that they will continue to be used selectively.

Reengineering. The use of reengineering programs and practices was not included in our earlier studies; thus, we cannot make a definitive statement about how rapidly it has grown. However, the adoption rate we found in 1996 clearly is very high, given the short history of process reengineering. The fact that 81 percent of the companies studied have a reengineering program is clear evidence that it has had a wide impact on Fortune 1000 corporations. If we had asked the same question in 1987 when we first studied employee involvement, it is likely that few, if any, companies would have responded that they had a reengineering program. They may have been using some of the practices associated with reengineering, since these were already available, but they were not likely to have a reengineering program.

Our results clearly show that the most popular reengineering practices are those that are likely to lead to cost reduction. These include using less supervision, doing the work with fewer individuals, and creating an overall lower cost structure. It is also clear that the major reason for adopting reengineering is cost reduction. For example, firms that have downsized and removed layers are particularly likely to adopt reengineering practices. As was true with employee involvement and TQM, the business strategy of the organization seems at least partly to be guiding the adoption of reengineering. Not surprisingly, such strategies include being a low-cost competitor and increasing the speed with which products are brought to market.

Finally, as was true with employee involvement and total quality management, reengineering seems to be adopted when particular improvement strategies are adopted. For example, focusing on core competencies, the adoption of information technology, and an emphasis on the competencies of employees are strongly associated with the adoption of reengineering practices. The adoption of reengineering is also strongly associated with integrated, clearly articulated and developed business and change strategies. Reengineering clearly is not something that tends to be adopted on its own but is typically part of an integrated change strategy. Although we must wait to find out whether reengineering's popularity will continue, our guess is that it will not, an opinion based on such factors as the bad press reengineering gets and its failure to pay attention to employee outcomes. Nevertheless, many of the practices associated with reengineering will probably continue to be adopted, since they have become "best practices" on their own.

Effectiveness of EI, TQM, and Reengineering. Across the board, virtually every company rates their employee involvement, total quality management, and reengineering efforts as successful. In the case of employee involvement, companies rate their reward system and power-sharing practices as highly successful. There is little tendency for programs to be rated more successful over their history. There is a trend, however, for programs to be rated as more successful as companies make greater use of the practices associated with that program. For example, in the case of employee involvement, more information sharing, more knowledge development, the adoption of more reward system practices, and the use of more power-sharing practices are all strongly associated with the perceived success of EI programs. Finally, the average EI outcome score is highest for the business involvement type.

There is a slight decrease in the overall satisfaction with total quality management from 1993 to 1996, but the programs are still rated as having a very positive impact on most outcomes, and there is a strong relationship between the amount of adoption and the success of the programs.

Despite the criticism of reengineering in many publications, the overall rating of reengineering is quite positive, and corporations see it as having generally positive impacts on a number of performance indicators. It too shows a strong relationship between its outcomes and the degree to which the practices associated with it are adopted.

The most interesting finding with respect to effectiveness concerns the interaction among EI, TQM, and reengineering. As a general rule, they seem to reinforce each other, increasing each other's effectiveness. This shows up in the tendency for the amount of adoption of any one of them to be associated with higher success ratings for the others. This strongly suggests that the most effective organizational change efforts are those that are able to integrate the practices commonly associated with EI, TQM, and reengineering.

Our results also show that several factors influence the effectiveness of employee involvement, total quality management, and reengineering programs. One of these, which we studied for the first time in 1996, is the nature of the employee contract. Particularly for EI and TQM, having the correct employment contract can contribute substantially to success. Emphasizing performance-based rewards and basing continued employment on performance are clearly associated with the effectiveness of EI and TQM programs.

An organization's change strategy also seems to be a clear determinant of how successful EI, TQM, and reengineering programs are. Change strategies that emphasize integrated, clearly articulated reasons for the direction of the change and that are led by top management seem to lead to successful EI, TQM, and reengineering programs. Since these are complicated programs to administer and implement, it is not surprising that the data do provide clear confirmation of the importance both of an overall strategic change agenda for a company and of this agenda being led by senior management. According to our findings, successful change seems less likely to come from a more bottom-up approach.

Perhaps the most important finding in the entire study is the relationship between the adoption of employee involvement, total quality management, and reengineering practices, and the financial performance of firms. Companies that adopt these approaches perform better, most likely because their adoption helps companies improve their performance. This conclusion is strongly supported by the results of this study, the most extensive ever done of the relationship between these practices and company financial performance. Particularly in the case of employee involvement practices, the performance difference between high and low users is so great that an overwhelming case exists for their adoption. Indeed, the argument can be made that companies that do not adopt employee involvement, total quality management, and reengineering practices are going to be at an increasingly large competitive disadvantage, foregoing millions of dollars in earnings and shareholder value.

Organizing in the Future. Our results leave little doubt that the shape of organizations has changed in the last decade. Corporations have reduced layers of management and have adopted a wide variety of practices that are associated with power sharing, quality improvement, and information technology. These changes have created a profoundly different work environment for employees, as well as a new employment contract. In some cases, these changes have led to a more skilled workforce and to extensive opportunities for employees to become more involved in the business. The changes also appear to have led to U.S. organizations toward becoming more competitive in the global economy.

It is quite likely that we are well on the way to inventing a new view of what constitutes effective organizational design and management. This new approach is not made up simply of employee involvement, or total quality management, or reengineering but rather of an integrated set of practices and structures that draw heavily from these three approaches. Thus, we seem to be heading toward a new logic of organizing that may ultimately lead to individuals and organizations thinking of employee involvement, total quality management, and reengineering as historical programs that helped shape this new management approach. If this occurs, then the individual programs may fade away, but such a scenario should not lead to the conclusion that these programs did not have an impact nor to the conclusion that their ideas, practices, and policies were not adopted. In many cases, quite the opposite may be true; that is, they have gone from being new policies and practices to standard operating procedures.

The data on the strategic nature of organizational change efforts lead us to be hopeful about the future. We see clear evidence that companies are aligning their business needs with their organizational structures and their management practices. They are increasingly integrating the key technical tools of TQM and reengineering with the employee involvement activities that can make these technical tools effective. Thus, there is a slow but steady movement toward reshaping organizations to focus more on performance capabilities and strategic directions and less on the creation of burdensome control structures and hierarchies.

In our 1995 book, we argued that the glass of organizational change is half empty or half full depending on one's perspective. In many respects, we still hold this opinion. Comparisons between 1987 and

1996 results show substantial change in the way U.S. corporations are managed. But in 1996, the number of employees covered by many of the best practices still remains surprisingly low given the performance improvements they produce.

We can document tremendous change, particularly with respect to employee involvement, but we can also document the fact that a tremendous number of employees are not yet well-trained participants in their business. We can also document that many of the change activities have been better for the organizations than they have been for the employees, largely because at least two of the major change efforts—total quality management and reengineering—do not seem to improve appreciably the satisfaction and well-being of employees. Organizations that have moved toward a widespread adoption of TQM and reengineering need to pay attention to the human side of the organization. In our opinion, this means focusing on key employee involvement practices and ensuring that the search for efficiency and competitive advantage does not overlook the key human assets that the organization needs to develop and maintain.

One encouraging note with respect to employee well-being is the emphasis that organizations seem to be placing on developing core competencies and the competencies of individuals. This suggests that organizations may increasingly realize that they have to do a good job of balancing the organizational needs for cost competitiveness and performance with the development of satisfying work relationships that can attract and hold individuals who are the source of competitive advantage.

If, as our results suggest, the most effective adoption of TQM, EI, and reengineering practices comes when an integrated package of these practices occurs, organizations may be just beginning to design themselves in the most effective ways. Few organizations at this point have consistently adopted the key elements of all three of these approaches on an organization-wide basis. In fact, a good guess is that few organizations cover even 10 percent of their employees with an integrated package of these practices.

Because of the relatively low use of multiple system change efforts, companies can still gain competitive advantage by being an early adopter not just of employee involvement or total quality management or reengineering but of an integrated set of practices that match business strategy, management practices, and change strategy. We believe that this is where competitive advantage lies in the future. Those companies that are able to put together the right pieces are likely to gain a significant long-term competitive advantage. Companies that wish to compete in a global environment must take an integrated, total systems approach to management. To do anything less creates a high risk of losing out to companies that are able to do it.

Our view of the future is fundamentally optimistic. Our research suggests that firms increasingly see that how they organize and how they deal with people are critical sources of competitive advantage. It confirms the accuracy of this view by showing that company financial performance is related to the adoption of EI, TQM, and reengineering. Research and practice are increasingly defining and clarifying the key elements of a high performance approach to management. This approach clearly includes many of the ideas and practices at the core of employee involvement, total quality management, and (perhaps to a lesser degree) reengineering.

Our research leads us to an interesting prediction: it will no longer be the degree to which companies have an effective TQM, EI, or reengineering program that is crucial for their success. Instead, it will be the degree to which they have an effective, integrated set of management practices that support their business strategy and their needs for particular core competencies and organizational capabilities. Indeed, we may be at the end of an era in which employee involvement, total quality management, and reengineering are popular "programs."But this is not to say that many of the practices and programs associated with these three approaches to management are likely to become any less popular or less important. Quite the opposite may be true as they become important elements in defining a new high performance approach to management that provides a significant competitive advantage and that in the future will be adopted by the most successful global corporations.

The Questionnaire

THE FOURTH NATIONAL SURVEY OF ORGANIZATIONAL PERFORMANCE IMPROVEMENT EFFORTS is being conducted by the University of Southern California. The purpose of this survey is to obtain information on the design, implementation, and operation of a variety of management practices and on employee involvement, total quality, and reengineering organizational improvement efforts.

This questionnaire is being sent to "Fortune 1000" corporations and should be answered by the CEO or someone else who is familiar with your corporation's management practices and organizational effectiveness efforts. Since this is a corporate-wide survey, the respondent may wish to consult key staff familiar with your improvement efforts throughout the corporation. Please answer the questions in terms of **employees in the United States only.** To clarify what is meant by the terms used in this questionnaire, a glossary is included.

Your response will be kept *confidential.* The questionnaire is numbered to aid us in our follow-up efforts and will not be used to single out you or your corporation. Your answers will be combined with those of other respondents and presented only in summary form in our report. Your response is voluntary; however, we urge you to respond since we cannot make a meaningful assessment of the Fortune 1000 without your survey.

This questionnaire should take about 30 minutes to complete. Most of the questions can be quickly answered by checking a box or circling a number. Please return the completed questionnaire in the enclosed postage-paid envelope within *21 days* of receipt. If you have any questions, please call Ed Lawler at (213) 740–9814.

In the event the return envelope is misplaced the address is:

Professor Edward E. Lawler III
Center for Effective Organizations
School of Business Administration
University of Southern California
Los Angeles, California 90089–1421

If you would like a complimentary copy of any of the following books, please indicate which books you want and print your name and complete mailing address or tape your business card below:

☐ Lawler, E., Mohrman, S. and Ledford, G., (1995). *Creating High Performance Organizations: Practices and Results of Employee Involvement and Total Quality Management in Fortune 1000 Companies.* Jossey-Bass San Francisco, CA (Report of our 1987, 1990 and 1993 studies).

☐ Mohrman, S., Cohen, S., and Mohrman, A. M., (1995). *Designing Team Based Organizations: New Forms of Knowledge Work.* Jossey-Bass, San Francisco, CA (A research based book on how to make teams effective).

☐ Lawler, E. E. III., (1996). *From the Ground Up: Six Principles for Creating New Logic Corporations.* Jossey-Bass, San Francisco, CA (A new book on organizational effectiveness).

_____

_____

_____

_____

_____

Thank you in advance for your participation in the study.

1. **What is the title or position of the individual completing the majority of this questionnaire? (Check one.)**

    ☐ 1. Chief Executive Officer, Chief Operating Officer, or President

    ☐ 2. Vice President for Human Resources, Industrial Relations, or Personnel (or equivalent title)

    ☐ 3. Vice President for function other than Human Resources, Industrial Relations, or Personnel (or equivalent title)

    ☐ 4. Corporate Manager for Operations (or equivalent title)

    ☐ 5. Director or Manager of Employee Involvement or Quality (or equivalent title)

    ☐ 6. Other (please specify) _____

2. **Of the total number of U.S. employees in your corporation, about what percent fall into each of the following categories?** *(Enter approximate percents, which should add to 100%.)*

    1. Hourly/clerical   _____%

    2. Technical/professional   _____%

    3. Supervisors/managers   _____%

    4. Other   _____%

              TOTAL   100%

3. **About what percent of your employees work in manufacturing operations?** *(Enter percent. If none, enter "0".)*

                    _____%

4. **About what percent of your corporation's non-managerial employees are represented by labor union(s)?** *(Enter percent. If none, enter "0".)*

                    _____%

5. **About what percent of your corporation's employees are employed in countries other than the United States?** *(Enter percent. If none, enter "0".)*

                    _____%

6. **Which of the following best describes your company?** *(Check one.)*

☐ 1. Single integrated business

☐ 2. Multiple related businesses with corporate functions providing some integrative support

☐ 3. Several sectors or groups of business units with some corporate functions and support

☐ 4. Multiple unrelated businesses managed independently in a "holding company" fashion

☐ 5. Multiple unrelated businesses actively managed by a corporate office

☐ 6. Other (please specify) _____

7. **Overall, to what extent is your corporation's business environment characterized by the following conditions:**

	Little or No Extent	Some Extent	Moderate Extent	Great Extent	Very Great Extent
1. Subject to heavy foreign competition	1	2	3	4	5
2. Rapidly growing market	1	2	3	4	5
3. Shorter product life cycles	1	2	3	4	5
4. Declining markets	1	2	3	4	5
5. Intense quality competition	1	2	3	4	5
6. Intense speed to market competition	1	2	3	4	5
7. Intense cost competition	1	2	3	4	5
8. Rapid change	1	2	3	4	5

	Little or No Extent	Some Extent	Moderate Extent	Great Extent	Very Great Extent

8. To what extent does your corporation's business strategy stress the following:

1. Increasing the percent of revenue from new products and services 1   2   3   4   5

2. Being a global company 1   2   3   4   5

3. Having a strong customer focus 1   2   3   4   5

4. Increasing the speed with which products are brought to market 1   2   3   4   5

5. Building knowledge and intellectual capital 1   2   3   4   5

6. Being a low cost competitor 1   2   3   4   5

7. Having high levels of quality in everything you do . . . 1   2   3   4   5

8. Responding quickly to changes in the market 1   2   3   4   5

9. Being a technology leader 1   2   3   4   5

9. Approximately how much has the size of your domestic (U.S.) workforce changed in the last ten years? *(Check one.)*

☐ 1. Decreased more than 50%   ☐ 8. Increased less than 20%

☐ 2. Decreased 41 to 50%   ☐ 9. Increased 21 to 40%

☐ 3. Decreased 31 to 40%   ☐ 10. Increased 41 to 60%

☐ 4. Decreased 21 to 30%   ☐ 11. Increased 61 to 80%

☐ 5. Decreased 10 to 20%   ☐ 12. Increased 81 to 100%

☐ 6. Decreased less than 10%   ☐ 13. Increased more than 100%

☐ 7. No change

10. **Has your corporation removed layers of management during the last ten years?** *(Check one.)*

    ☐ 1. Yes

    ☐ 2. No (If no, please go to question 12)

11. **If yes, how many layers of management were removed?** *(Check one.)*

    ☐ 1. One   ☐ 4. Four

    ☐ 2. Two   ☐ 5. Five

    ☐ 3. Three   ☐ 6. Six or More

12. **Does your organization have a formal statement of the social or employment contract that defines what it expects of employees and what they can expect in return?** *(Check one.)*

    ☐ 1. Yes

    ☐ 2. No (If no, please go to question 14)

13. **If you have a formal written contract, is it . . .** *(Pick the most appropriate answer.)*

    ☐ 1. New in the last three years and valid

    ☐ 2. New in the last three years but not valid

    ☐ 3. More than three years old and still valid

    ☐ 4. More than three years old and badly out of date

14. To what extent do the following describe the employment contract your corporation currently operates by (whether written or not)?

	Little or No Extent	Some Extent	Moderate Extent	Great Extent	Very Great Extent
1. Career development is the responsibility of the individual	1	2	3	4	5
2. The continued employment of individuals is based on their performance	1	2	3	4	5
3. The continued employment of individuals is based on their continuing to develop their skills and knowledge	1	2	3	4	5
4. Rewards are tied to seniority	1	2	3	4	5
5. Loyalty to the company is rewarded	1	2	3	4	5
6. Outstanding performers have a job for life	1	2	3	4	5
7. Rewards are tied to individual performance	1	2	3	4	5
8. Rewards are tied to group and/or organization performance	1	2	3	4	5
9. Employees are expected to manage their own performance with a minimum of supervision	1	2	3	4	5
10. No one has a secure job	1	2	3	4	5
11. Fits the corporate business strategy	1	2	3	4	5
12. Is understood by most employees	1	2	3	4	5
13. Employees are satisfied with it	1	2	3	4	5
14. We are changing direction so fast, it is not clear what the contract is	1	2	3	4	5

15. Are you currently working on developing a new statement of your corporation's employment contract? (*Check one.*)

☐ 1. Yes

☐ 2. No

☐ 3. Not sure

This section asks questions about your corporation's information sharing, training, reward system, and employee involvement practices. (Items with an asterisk are defined in the glossary.)

INFORMATION SHARING

	None (0%)	Almost None (1–20%)	Some (21–40%)	About Half (41–60%)	Most (61–80%)	Almost All (81–99%)	All (100%)
1. About how many corporation employees are routinely provided with the following types of information?							
1. Information about the corporation's overall operating results	1	2	3	4	5	6	7
2. Information about their *unit's* operating results	1	2	3	4	5	6	7
3. Advance information on new technologies that may affect them	1	2	3	4	5	6	7
4. Information on business plans/goals	1	2	3	4	5	6	7
5. Information on competitors' relative performance	1	2	3	4	5	6	7

TRAINING

2. **About how many corporation employees have received, within the past 3 years, systematic, formal training on the following types of skills?**

	None (0%)	Almost None (1–20%)	Some (21–40%)	About Half (41–60%)	Most (61–80%)	Almost All (81–99%)	All (100%)
1. Group decision-making/problem-solving skills	1	2	3	4	5	6	7
2. Leadership skills	1	2	3	4	5	6	7
3. Skills in understanding the business (accounting, finance, etc.)	1	2	3	4	5	6	7
4. Quality/statistical analysis skills	1	2	3	4	5	6	7
5. Team building skills	1	2	3	4	5	6	7
6. Job skills training	1	2	3	4	5	6	7
7. Cross training	1	2	3	4	5	6	7

PAY/REWARD SYSTEM

	None (0%)	Almost None (1–20%)	Some (21–40%)	About Half (41–60%)	Most (61–80%)	Almost All (81–99%)	All (100%)
3. About how many employees are covered by or are eligible for a pay/reward system with each of the following elements?							
1. All-salaried pay systems*	1	2	3	4	5	6	7
2. Knowledge/skill-based pay*	1	2	3	4	5	6	7
3. Profit sharing*	1	2	3	4	5	6	7
4. Gainsharing*	1	2	3	4	5	6	7
5. Individual incentives*	1	2	3	4	5	6	7
6. Work group or team incentives*	1	2	3	4	5	6	7
7. Non-monetary recognition awards for performance*	1	2	3	4	5	6	7
8. Employee stock ownership plan*	1	2	3	4	5	6	7
9. Flexible, cafeteria-style benefits*	1	2	3	4	5	6	7
10. Employment security*	1	2	3	4	5	6	7
11. Open pay information*	1	2	3	4	5	6	7
12. Stock option plan*	1	2	3	4	5	6	7

INVOLVEMENT PRACTICES

	None (0%)	Almost None (1–20%)	Some (21–40%)	About Half (41–60%)	Most (61–80%)	Almost All (81–99%)	All (100%)
4. About how many of your corporation's employees are currently involved in each of the following activities or programs?							
1. Suggestion system*	1	2	3	4	5	6	7
2. Survey feedback*	1	2	3	4	5	6	7
3. Job enrichment or redesign*	1	2	3	4	5	6	7
4. Quality circles*	1	2	3	4	5	6	7
5. Employee participation groups other than quality circles*	1	2	3	4	5	6	7
6. Union-management quality of work life (QWL) committees*	1	2	3	4	5	6	7
7. Mini-business units*	1	2	3	4	5	6	7
8. Self-managing work teams*	1	2	3	4	5	6	7
9. Employee committees concerned with policy and/or strategy*	1	2	3	4	5	6	7

Here, we ask about the extent to which your corporation uses certain *patterns* of employee involvement practices.

1. **Approximately what percent of your corporation's employees are in units in which each of the following patterns of employee involvement practice is predominant? Please allocate 100% in answering 1–5.**

   _____%   1. **None.** No significant employee involvement exists in these parts of the corporation.

   _____%   2. **Improvement Teams.** Employee involvement focuses on special groups that are responsible for recommending improvements to management. These groups may be participation groups, quality circles, quality action teams, union-management QWL committees, etc. Members of the groups receive special training to enable them to work better as a team. They receive information relevant to the problems they are working on. There may be financial rewards or recognition for team suggestions.

   _____%   3. **Job Involvement.** Employee involvement focuses on creating work designs that are highly motivating, such as self-managing teams. Training focuses on job-specific skills and/or team functioning. Employees receive information relevant to their performance as individuals and/or teams. The reward system may reinforce the job design emphasis; practices might include team performance incentives or pay increases for mastering skills that are needed within a team.

   _____%   4. **Business Involvement.** Employees are involved heavily in the management of the business. Improvement teams and job involvement approaches may be used as part of this strategy. Self-managing work teams and perhaps mini-business units are used extensively, and management routinely seeks employee input on policies and practices of the organization. Reward innovations are used, perhaps including gainsharing or profit sharing in the unit. Employees receive extensive training in job skills, team skills, and in business issues. Employees receive extensive business information and they are expected to use it.

   _____%   5. **Other Form of Involvement.** Employee involvement approaches not described by 2, 3, or 4.

NOTE: PERCENTAGES SHOULD ADD TO 100%

This section asks you to evaluate your corporation's practices.

1. How successful or unsuccessful do you think each of the following is in terms of impact on improving your organization's performance? **DO NOT ANSWER FOR ANY PRACTICE YOU DO NOT HAVE IN YOUR ORGANIZATION.**

PAY/REWARD SYSTEM

	Very Unsuccessful	Unsuccessful	Undecided	Successful	Very Successful
1. All-salaried pay systems	1	2	3	4	5
2. Knowledge/skill-based pay	1	2	3	4	5
3. Profit sharing	1	2	3	4	5
4. Gainsharing	1	2	3	4	5
5. Individual incentives	1	2	3	4	5
6. Work group or team incentives	1	2	3	4	5
7. Non-monetary recognition awards for performance	1	2	3	4	5
8. Employee stock ownership plan	1	2	3	4	5
9. Flexible, cafeteria-style benefits	1	2	3	4	5
10. Employment security	1	2	3	4	5
11. Open pay information	1	2	3	4	5
12. Stock option plan	1	2	3	4	5

INVOLVEMENT PRACTICES

	Very Unsuccessful	Unsuccessful	Undecided	Successful	Very Successful
1. Suggestion system	1	2	3	4	5
2. Survey feedback	1	2	3	4	5
3. Job enrichment or redesign	1	2	3	4	5
4. Quality circles	1	2	3	4	5
5. Employee participation groups other than quality circles	1	2	3	4	5
6. Union-management quality of work life (QWL) committees	1	2	3	4	5
7. Mini-business units	1	2	3	4	5
8. Self-managing work teams	1	2	3	4	5
9. Employee committees concerned with policy and/or strategy	1	2	3	4	5

This section asks questions about your corporation's employee involvement efforts. By "employee involvement" we do not mean one specific innovation and program. Rather, we refer to the full range of innovations and programs that may involve employees in decisions affecting their work and work environment.

1. To what extent, if at all, are unions involved in your corporation's employee involvement efforts? *(Check one.)*

☐ 0. No unions (not applicable)

☐ 1. Little or no extent

☐ 2. Some extent

☐ 3. Moderate extent

☐ 4. Great extent

☐ 5. Very great extent

2. How much of a negative or positive impact, if either, have employee involvement efforts had on each of the following performance indicators in your corporation?

	Very Negative	Negative	Neither	Positive	Very Positive	No Basis to Judge
1. Productivity	1	2	3	4	5	0
2. Quality of product or services	1	2	3	4	5	0
3. Customer service	1	2	3	4	5	0
4. Employee satisfaction	1	2	3	4	5	0
5. Turnover	1	2	3	4	5	0
6. Absenteeism	1	2	3	4	5	0
7. Competitiveness	1	2	3	4	5	0
8. Profitability	1	2	3	4	5	0
9. Employee quality of work life	1	2	3	4	5	0
10. Speed	1	2	3	4	5	0
11. Employee loyalty	1	2	3	4	5	0

3. To what extent, if at all, have employee involvement efforts resulted in each of the following internal business conditions?

	Little or No Extent	Some Extent	Moderate Extent	Great Extent	Very Great Extent	Don't Know
1. Eliminated layers of management or supervision	1	2	3	4	5	6
2. Changed management style to one that is more participatory	1	2	3	4	5	6
3. Improved union-management relations	1	2	3	4	5	6
4. Moved decision-making authority to lower organizational level	1	2	3	4	5	6
5. Moved performance-based rewards to lower organizational levels	1	2	3	4	5	6
6. Broadened skill development at lower organizational levels	1	2	3	4	5	6
7. Increased information flow throughout the corporation	1	2	3	4	5	6
8. Increased employee trust in management . . .	1	2	3	4	5	6
9. Improved management decision-making . . .	1	2	3	4	5	6
10. Improved employee safety/health	1	2	3	4	5	6
11. Improved organizational processes and procedures	1	2	3	4	5	6

4. Overall how positive has your experience been with your employee involvement efforts?

☐ 1. Very Negative

☐ 2. Negative

☐ 3. Neither Negative nor Positive

☐ 4. Positive

☐ 5. Very Positive

This section asks about your total quality efforts.

1. **About what percent of employees in your corporation are covered by Total Quality Control (TQC), Total Quality Management (TQM), or similar quality efforts?**

_____%

(IF THE ANSWER IS 0, TURN TO PAGE 13)

2. **When did your quality programs start in relation to your employee involvement activities?**

   ☐ 1. Employee involvement started first

   ☐ 2. Both started simultaneously

   ☐ 3. Quality improvement programs started first

3. **How are they managed?**

   ☐ 1. Two separate programs

   ☐ 2. Two separate but coordinated programs

   ☐ 3. One integrated program

4. About how many employees work in units that use the following practices?

	None (0%)	Almost None (1-20%)	Some (21-40%)	About Half (41-60%)	Most (61-80%)	Almost All (81-99%)	All (100%)
1. Quality improvement teams	1	2	3	4	5	6	7
2. Quality councils	1	2	3	4	5	6	7
3. Cross-functional planning (e.g., Quality Functional Deployment)	1	2	3	4	5	6	7
4. Direct employee exposure to customers	1	2	3	4	5	6	7
5. Self-inspection	1	2	3	4	5	6	7
6. Work simplification	1	2	3	4	5	6	7
7. Cost of quality monitoring	1	2	3	4	5	6	7
8. Customer satisfaction monitoring	1	2	3	4	5	6	7
9. Collaboration with suppliers in quality efforts	1	2	3	4	5	6	7
10. Just-in-time deliveries	1	2	3	4	5	6	7
11. Work cells or manufacturing cells	1	2	3	4	5	6	7
12. Statistical control methods used by front-line employees	1	2	3	4	5	6	7

5. Which statement comes closest to describing how the majority of managers in your organization think about your quality and employee involvement activities?

☐ 1. Employee involvement is an important part of our quality program activities.

☐ 2. Quality activities are an important part of our employee involvement activities.

6. How much of a negative or positive impact, if either, have your total quality management efforts had on each of the following performance indicators in your corporation?

	Very Negative	Negative	Neither	Positive	Very Positive	No Basis to Judge
1. Productivity	1	2	3	4	5	0
2. Quality of product or services	1	2	3	4	5	0
3. Customer service	1	2	3	4	5	0
4. Employee satisfaction	1	2	3	4	5	0
5. Turnover	1	2	3	4	5	0
6. Absenteeism	1	2	3	4	5	0
7. Competitiveness	1	2	3	4	5	0
8. Profitability	1	2	3	4	5	0
9. Employee quality of work life	1	2	3	4	5	0
10. Speed	1	2	3	4	5	0
11. Employee loyalty	1	2	3	4	5	0

7. **In the next 3 years, how will your corporation's use of TQM change?** *(Check one.)*

☐ 1. Greatly decrease   ☐ 4. Increase

☐ 2. Decrease   ☐ 5. Greatly increase

☐ 3. Stay the same

8. **To what extent, if at all, are unions involved in your corporation's TQM efforts?** *(Check one.)*

☐ 0. No unions (not applicable)

☐ 1. Little or no extent   ☐ 4. Great extent

☐ 2. Some extent   ☐ 5. Very great extent

☐ 3. Moderate extent

9. **Overall how positive has your experience been with your total quality management efforts?**
   (Check one.)

   ☐ 1. Very Negative

   ☐ 2. Negative

   ☐ 3. Neither Negative nor Positive

   ☐ 4. Positive

   ☐ 5. Very Positive

This section asks about your process reengineering activities.

1. **About what percent of employees in your corporation work in units that have had process reengineering efforts?**

_____%

(IF THE ANSWER IS 0, PLEASE SKIP TO PAGE 15)

2. **To what extent, have your process reengineering efforts resulted in the following?**

	Little or No Extent	Some Extent	Moderate Extent	Great Extent	Very Great Extent
1. Process simplification	1	2	3	4	5
2. The creation of cross-functional units (e.g., departments, customer or product focused units)	1	2	3	4	5
3. Major information system redesign	1	2	3	4	5
4. Enriched multi-skilled _individual_ jobs	1	2	3	4	5
5. Multi-skilled _teams_	1	2	3	4	5
6. Doing the same work with fewer people	1	2	3	4	5
7. Doing the same work with less supervision	1	2	3	4	5
8. A lower overall cost structure	1	2	3	4	5

3. How much of a negative or positive impact, if either, have your process reengineering efforts had on each of the following performance indicators in your corporation?

	Very Negative	Negative	Neither	Positive	Very Positive	No Basis to Judge
1. Productivity	1	2	3	4	5	0
2. Quality of product or services	1	2	3	4	5	0
3. Customer service	1	2	3	4	5	0
4. Employee satisfaction	1	2	3	4	5	0
5. Turnover	1	2	3	4	5	0
6. Absenteeism	1	2	3	4	5	0
7. Competitiveness	1	2	3	4	5	0
8. Profitability	1	2	3	4	5	0
9. Employee quality of work life	1	2	3	4	5	0
10. Speed	1	2	3	4	5	0
11. Employee loyalty	1	2	3	4	5	0

4. **Which of the following best describes your reengineering efforts?** *(Check one.)*

☐ 1. A separate program

☐ 2. Integrated with our quality and involvement efforts

☐ 3. Integrated with our quality efforts but *not* our involvement efforts

☐ 4. Integrated with our involvement efforts but *not* our quality efforts

5. **Overall how positive has your experience been with your process reengineering efforts?** *(Check one.)*

☐ 1. Very Negative

☐ 2. Negative

☐ 3. Neither Negative nor Positive

☐ 4. Positive

☐ 5. Very Positive

This section asks about the overall approach your corporation is taking to performance improvement.

1. To what extent are you using the following in your organizational performance improvement efforts?	Little or No Extent	Some Extent	Moderate Extent	Great Extent	Very Great Extent
1. Creating global business units	1	2	3	4	5
2. Building a team-based organization	1	2	3	4	5
3. Using temporary project teams to perform core work	1	2	3	4	5
4. Focusing on core competencies	1	2	3	4	5
5. Outsourcing work that is not one of your core competencies or can be done more cheaply externally	1	2	3	4	5
6. Reducing the size of the corporate staff	1	2	3	4	5
7. Introducing new performance measures	1	2	3	4	5
8. Restructuring the corporation by creating new units and eliminating existing ones	1	2	3	4	5
9. Reducing the number of different businesses you are in	1	2	3	4	5
10. Emphasizing the competencies of employees	1	2	3	4	5
11. Significant adoption of new information technology . . .	1	2	3	4	5

2. To what extent are the following descriptive
of your organizational performance
improvement efforts?

	Little or No Extent	Some Extent	Moderate Extent	Great Extent	Very Great Extent
1. Guided by a clearly stated business strategy	1	2	3	4	5
2. Guided by clearly stated beliefs about what makes an organization effective	1	2	3	4	5
3. Integrated company-wide	1	2	3	4	5
4. Occurring quite differently in different business units . .	1	2	3	4	5
5. Driven by a threat to the organization's survival	1	2	3	4	5
6. Guided by a mission and values statement	1	2	3	4	5
7. Led by top management	1	2	3	4	5
8. Based on a bottom up implementation strategy	1	2	3	4	5
9. The same no matter what country employees work in	1	2	3	4	5
10. Made up of a series of unrelated initiatives	1	2	3	4	5
11. Based on a three or more year plan	1	2	3	4	5

PAY/REWARD SYSTEMS

1. **All-salaried pay systems:** A system in which all employees are salaried, thus eliminating the distinction between hourly and salaried employees.

2. **Knowledge/skill-based pay:** An alternative to traditional job-based pay that sets pay levels based on how many skills employees have or how many jobs they potentially can do, not on the job they are currently holding. Also called pay for skills, pay for knowledge, and competency-based pay.

3. **Profit sharing:** A bonus plan that shares some portion of corporation profits with employees. It does not include dividend sharing.

4. **Gainsharing:** Gainsharing plans are based on a formula that shares some portion of gains in productivity, quality, cost effectiveness, or other performance indicators. The gains are shared in the form of bonuses with all employees in an organization (such as a plant). It typically includes a system of employee suggestion committees. It differs from profit sharing and an ESOP in that the basis of the formula is some set of local performance measures, not corporation profits. Examples include the Scanlon Plan, the Improshare Plan, the Rucker Plan, and various custom-designed plans.

5. **Individual incentives:** Bonuses or other financial compensation tied to short-term or long-term individual performance.

6. **Work group or team incentives:** Bonuses or other financial compensation tied to short-term or long-term work group, permanent team, or temporary team performance.

7. **Non-monetary recognition awards for performance:** Any non-monetary reward (including gifts, publicity, dinners, etc.) for individual or group performance.

8. **Employee stock ownership plan:** A credit mechanism that enables employees to buy their employer's stock, thus giving them

an ownership stake in the corporation; the stock is held in trust until employees quit or retire.

9. **Flexible, cafeteria-style benefits:** A plan that gives employees choices in the types and amounts of various fringe benefits they receive.

10. **Employment security:** Corporation policy designed to prevent layoffs.

11. **Open pay information:** A communication program that gives employees information about pay policies, ranges, increase amounts, bonus amounts, and job or skill evaluation systems. May or may not include information about what specific individuals are paid.

12. **Stock option plan:** A plan that gives employees the opportunity to purchase company stock at a previously established price.

INVOLVEMENT PRACTICES

1. **Suggestion system:** A program that elicits individual employee suggestions on improving work or the work environment.

2. **Survey feedback:** Use of employee attitude survey results, not simply as an employee opinion poll, but rather as part of a larger problem-solving process in which survey data are used to encourage, structure, and measure the effectiveness of employee participation.

3. **Job enrichment or redesign:** Design of work that is intended to increase worker performance and job satisfaction by increasing skill variety, autonomy, significance and identity of the task, and performance feedback.

4. **Quality circles:** Structured type of employee participation groups in which groups of volunteers from a particular work area meet regularly to identify and suggest improvements to work-related problems. The goals of QCs are improved quality and productivity; there are no direct rewards for circle activity, group problem-solving training is provided, and the groups' only power is to suggest changes to management.

5. **Employee participation groups other than quality circles:** Any employee participation group, such as task teams or employee work

councils, that does not fall within the definitions of either self-managing work teams or quality circles.

6. **Union-management quality of work life (QWL):** Joint union-management committees, usually existing at multiple organizational levels, alongside the established union and management relationships and collective bargaining committees. QWL committees usually are prohibited from directly addressing contractual issues such as pay, and are charged with developing changes that improve both organizational performance and employee quality of work life.

7. **Mini-business units:** Relatively small, self-contained organizational unit (perhaps smaller than the plant level) that produces its own product of service and operates in a decentralized, partly autonomous fashion as a small business.

8. **Self-managing work teams:** Also termed autonomous work groups, semi-autonomous work groups, self-regulating work teams, or simply work teams. The work group (in some cases, acting without a supervisor) is responsible for a whole product or service and makes decisions about task assignments and work methods. The team may be responsible for its own support services such as maintenance, purchasing, and quality control and may perform certain personnel functions such as hiring and firing team members and determining pay increases.

9. **Employee committees concerned with policy and/or strategy:** Any group or committee that includes non-management employees that is created to comment on, offer advice on, or determine major corporation policies and/or business strategies.

Construction and Calculation of Index Scores

Beginning in Section Seven, we present results based on index scores for employee involvement and each element of employee involvement (information sharing, knowledge, rewards, and power sharing). We also present results based on index scores for total quality management and reengineering. This appendix provides additional information about how the indices were constructed and calculated. Our description is aimed at interested readers who want enough information to understand our procedures, but not at academic colleagues who are interested in highly technical statistical details about the indices.

Our indices of management practices are somewhat different from standard survey scales, such as job satisfaction, pay equity, or work group conflict. These measures typically are constituted of multiple survey items. Researchers use statistical tests, such as factor analysis and internal consistency reliability analysis, to demonstrate that these items are reliable indicators of the same underlying construct. The items in the measure covary—that is, the scores on all items are highly correlated. Management practices are different because they are partly substitutable. For example, an organization that includes all employees in quality circles probably will not also include all employees in participation groups or union-management QWL committees. However, other practices, such as communication of different kinds of information, may covary as in a traditional survey scale.

Thus, we used a three-step procedure to develop appropriate indices. First, we used standard statistical procedures (factor analysis and internal consistency reliability analysis) to discover practices that when combined represented different indicators of the same underlying construct. The information-sharing practices, for instance, all loaded highly on the same factor and had a high reliability score. The same is true for three social skills training items: namely, training in group decision-making and problem-solving skills, training in leadership skills, and training in team-building skills. Items with these characteristics were averaged into scales or subscales.

Second, we used items relevant to each of the four major constructs that were strongly relevant theoretically and that were at least to some extent related statistically to other items in that index.

Finally, we made sure that our measures of power, rewards, information, and knowledge were appropriate in all four time periods (1987, 1990, 1993, and 1996). Because we are interested in examining changes over time, we did not include in the indices items that were new in the 1993 survey. These included stock option plans and employee committees concerned with policy or strategy.

The indices reported in this book are slightly different from those we reported in our study of the 1990 data (Lawler and others, 1992). We dropped the weightings used for some items in order to simplify the indices. Changes in the mix of practices that companies used in 1993 led to new patterns in the relationship of practices within each index. We also revised the indices so that they would be both meaningful and consistent across all four time periods.

Employee Involvement Indices We calculated the *information* index score for each company that was the average of the company's scores for all information-sharing practices. These are the same items that we used for the information index in previous years.

We calculated a *knowledge* index score for each firm that averaged the scores for the social skills training subscale, training in skills in understanding the business, quality/statistical analysis, job skills, and cross-training. We used all of these items in the knowledge indices we constructed in previous years, although we used a different formula for combining these items.

We calculated a *rewards* index score for each firm that averaged scores for four key reward practices that research has indicated are related both to other employee involvement practices and to organizational effectiveness. These reward practices were knowledge- or skill-based pay, profit sharing, gainsharing, and employee stock ownership plans. We dropped two items that were not used in the 1987 survey (work-group or team incentives and nonmonetary awards), one practice that research has not clearly demonstrated to impact organizational effectiveness (all-salaried pay systems), and one practice that is important but is not necessarily supportive of employee involvement efforts (individual incentives).

We calculated a *power* index score for each firm that averaged the firm's scores on survey feedback, job enrichment, quality circles, participation groups, union-management QWL committees, minibusiness units, and self-managing work teams. We dropped the use of two subscales present in our prior study because there was a different pattern in the data in 1993. We excluded suggestion systems from the index on statistical grounds. We excluded employee policy and strategy committees because this was a new item in 1993.

The *employee involvement index* score was obtained by averaging the index scores for each of the four constituent elements of employee involvement—that is, information, knowledge, rewards, and power. Each of the four indices was weighted equally.

Total Quality Management Indices Our statistical analyses indicated that there were two meaningful TQM scales. *Core practices* consisted of quality improvement teams, quality councils, cross-functional planning, customer satisfaction monitoring, collaboration with suppliers in quality efforts, and direct employee exposure to customers. *Production-oriented practices* included statistical control methods used by front-line employees, self-inspection, and work or manufacturing scales. Two single items did not fit with either scale: just-in-time deliveries and work simplification.

Meaning of Scale Scores A score on any of these indices may be thought of as representing the degree of employee coverage (measured on a seven-point scale) for the average practice included in the index. The response scale for these items refers to specific percentages of employees who are covered by the practice. For example, an index score of 3.0 corresponds to the point on the scale indicating that between 21 and 40 percent of employees are covered by the average information-sharing practice. Thus, the index scores have a concrete meaning.

Reengineerng Indices Our statistical analyses indicated that there were two meaningful reengineering scales. The *work structure* index included five items, all of which described approaches to organization and work designs. The *cost reengineering* index contains three items, two of which involved eliminating employees and one that referred to other cost reductions. The response scales for these items were extent-of-use ratings ranging from 1 (little or no) to 5 (great). Thus, a high scale score means heavy use.

References

Beer, M., Eisenstat, R. A., and Spector, B. (1990). Why change programs don't produce change. *Harvard Business Review 68*(6): 158–66.

Blasi, J. R. (1988). *Employee ownership: Revolution or rip-off?* Cambridge, Mass.: Ballinger.

Blinder, A. S. (1990). *Paying for productivity.* Washington, D.C.: Brookings.

Bluestone, B., and Bluestone, I. (1992). *Negotiating the future.* New York: Basic Books.

Collins, J. C., and Porras, J. I. (1994). *Built to last.* New York: Harper Business.

Commission on the Skills of the American Workforce. (1990). *America's choice: High skill or low wages!* Rochester, N.Y.: National Center on Education and the Economy.

Cotton, J. L., Vollrath, D. A., Froggatt, K. L., Lengnick-Hall, M. L., and Jennings, K. R. (1988). Employee participation: Diverse forms and different outcomes. *Academy of Management Review 13*(1): 8–22.

Davenport, T. H. (1993). *Process innovation: Re-engineering work through information technology.* Boston: Harvard Business School Press.

Deming, W. E. (1986). *Out of the crisis.* Cambridge, Mass.: MIT Press.

Denison, D. R. (1990). *Corporate culture and organizational effectiveness.* New York: Wiley.

Dertouzos, M. L., Lester, R. R., and Solow, R. M. (1989). *Made in America: Regaining the production edge.* Cambridge, Mass.: MIT Press.

Doyle, R. J., and Doyle, P. I. (1992). *Gain management.* New York: AMA.

Golembiewski, R. T., and Sun, G. (1990). QWL improves worksite quality: Success rates in a large pool of studies. *Human Resource Development Quarterly, 1*(1), 35–44.

Hackman, J. R., and Oldham, G. R. (1980). *Work redesign.* Reading, Mass.: Addison-Wesley.

Hamel, G. (1994). The concept of core competence. In G. Hamel and A. Heene (eds.), *Competence-based competition.* New York: Wiley.

Hammer, M. (1990). Reengineering work: Don't automate, obliterate. *Harvard Business Review 90*(4), 104–13.

Hammer, M., and Champy, J. (1993). *Reengineering the corporation.* New York: Harper Business Press.

Hansen, G. S., and Wernerfelt, B. (1989). Determinants of firm performance: The relative importance of economic and organizational factors. *Strategic Management Journal, 10,* 399–411.

Herrick, N. (1990). *Joint management and employee participation: Labor and management at the crossroads.* San Francisco: Jossey-Bass.

Herzberg, F. (1966). *Work and the nature of man.* Cleveland, Ohio: World.

Huselid, M. A. (1995). The impact of human resources management practices on turnover, productivity, and corporate financial performance. *Academy of Management Journal, 38,* 635–72.

Huselid, M. A., and Becker, B. B. (1996). Methodological issues in cross-sectional and panel estimates of the human resources–firm performance link. *Industrial Relations, 35,* 400–22.

Ichniowski, C., Kochan, T. A., Levine, D., Olson, C., and Strauss, G. (1996). What works at work. *Industrial Relations, 35,* 299–333.

Juran, J. M. (1989). *Juran on leadership for quality.* New York: Free Press.

Kochan, T. A. and Osterman, P. (1994). *The mutual gains enterprise.* Boston: Harvard Business School Press.

Kotter, J. P. (1997). *Leading change.* New York: Free Press.

Kotter, J. P., and Heskett, J. L. (1992). *Corporate culture and performance.* New York: Free Press.

Lawler, E. E. (1986). *High-involvement management.* San Francisco: Jossey-Bass.

Lawler, E. E. (1990). *Strategic pay: Aligning organizational strategies and pay systems.* San Francisco: Jossey-Bass.

Lawler, E. E. (1992). *The ultimate advantage.* San Francisco: Jossey-Bass.

Lawler, E. E. (1994). Total quality management and employee involvement: Are they compatible? *Academy of Management Executive 8*(1): 68–76.

Lawler, E. E. (1996). *From the ground up: Six principles for creating new logic organizations.* San Francisco: Jossey-Bass.

Lawler, E. E., and Cohen, S. G. (1992). Designing pay systems for teams. *ACA Journal 1*(1): 6–19.

Lawler, E. E., Ledford, G. E., Jr., and Mohrman, S. A. (1989). *Employee involvement in America: A study of contemporary practice.* Houston: American Productivity and Quality Center.

Lawler, E. E., and Mohrman, S. A. (1985). Quality circles after the fad. *Harvard Business Review 63*(1): 64–71.

Lawler, E. E., Mohrman, S. A., and Ledford, G. E., Jr. (1992). *Employee involvement and total quality management: Practices and results in Fortune 1000 companies.* San Francisco: Jossey-Bass.

Lawler, E. E., Mohrman, S. A., and Ledford, G. E., Jr. (1995). *Creating high performance organizations: Practices and results of employee involvement and total quality management in Fortune 1000 companies.* San Francisco: Jossey-Bass.

Ledford, G. E., Jr. (1991). Three case studies on skill-based pay: An overview. *Compensation and Benefits Review* 23(2): 11–23.

Ledford, G. E., Lawler, E. E., and Mohrman, S. A. (1988). The quality circle and its variations. In J. P. Campbell and R. J. Campbell (eds.), *Productivity in organizations: New perspectives from industrial and organizational psychology.* San Francisco: Jossey-Bass.

MacDuffie, J. P., and Krafcik, J. F. (1992). Integrating technology and human resources for high performance manufacturing: Evidence from the international auto industry. In T. A. Kochan and Michael Useem (eds.), *Transforming organizations.* New York: Oxford University Press.

Mills, D. Q. (1991). *Rebirth of the corporation.* New York: Wiley.

Mohrman, S. A., Cohen, S. G., and Mohrman, A. M. (1995). *Designing team-based organizations: New forms for knowledge work.* San Francisco: Jossey-Bass.

Mohrman, S. A., Galbraith, J. A., and Lawler, E. E. (1998). *Tomorrow's organization: Crafting winning capabilities in a dynamic world.* San Francisco: Jossey-Bass.

Mohrman, A. M., Jr., Mohrman, S. A., Ledford, G. E., Lawler, E. E., and Cummings, T. G. (1989). *Large-scale organizational change.* San Francisco: Jossey-Bass.

Moran, L., Hogeveen, J., Latham, J. and Ross-Eft, D. (1994). *Winning competitive advantage: A blended strategy works best.* Cupertino, Calif.: Zenger-Miller.

Nadler, D. A., Shaw, R. B., Walton, A. E., and Associates. (1995). *Discontinuous change.* San Francisco: Jossey-Bass.

O'Dell, C. (1987). *People, performance, and pay.* Houston, Texas: American Productivity Center.

O'Toole, J. (1995). *Leading change.* San Francisco: Jossey-Bass.

Peters, T. J., and Waterman, R. H. (1982). *In search of excellence.* New York: Harper Collins.

Pfeffer, J. (1994). *Competitive advantage through people.* Boston: Harvard Business School Press.

Prahalad, C. K., and Hamel, G. (1990). The core competence of the corporation. *Harvard Business Review* 68(3): 79–91.

Reich, R. B. (1991). *The work of nations.* New York: Knopf.

Rogers, E. M. (1983). *Diffusion of innovations* (3rd ed.). New York: Free Press.